The Anglo-Norman Dialect

Columbia University

STUDIES IN ROMANCE PHILOLOGY AND LITERATURE

THE ANGLO-NORMAN DIALECT

THE

ANGLO-NORMAN DIALECT

A MANUAL OF ITS
PHONOLOGY AND MORPHOLOGY

WITH ILLUSTRATIVE SPECIMENS OF THE LITERATURE

BY

LOUIS EMIL MENGER, Ph.D.
LATE PROFESSOR OF ROMANCE PHILOLOGY IN BRYN MAWR COLLEGE

New York

THE COLUMBIA UNIVERSITY PRESS

THE MACMILLAN COMPANY, Agents
LONDON: MACMILLAN & CO., Ltd.

1904

PREFATORY NOTE

IN view of the circumstances attending the appearance of this work, it has been thought appropriate to give it in some degree the form of a memorial volume. One of the author's close friends and associates has been asked to prepare a brief biographical notice, and a likeness of Dr. Menger, introduced as a frontispiece, will enhance the interest of the book to his many friends. A large part of the work had received the benefit of the author's revision in the proofs; but it remained for the editor a very special duty of love and friendship to exercise the patient vigilance requisite to seeing accurately through the final stages of the press a work so bristling with technicalities and minute details. In particular it devolved upon the editor to seek out, insert, and verify the array of cross-references called for in blank, but not indicated in the main in the author's manuscript nor in the early proofs. Owing to the peculiar nature of the presentation, it was not found to be feasible or desirable to provide an index in the ordinary sense of the word, but it is thought that the detailed analytical table of contents will serve every necessary purpose. It was not a part of Professor Menger's plan to supply a vocabulary and notes to the illustrative extracts. The exposition of these passages, so far as called for, was intended to be given by the professor in charge of the course of study.

In the belief that the amount of highly specialized and skilful labor bestowed by Dr. Menger on the task of his predilection will be found abundantly justified by the degree of its usefulness to all students of Anglo-Norman, — even to those most thoroughly versed in this broadly important field, — the book is confidently offered as the partially fulfilled promise of an undertaking and of a career prematurely cut off in the freshness of youthful vigor and fruition.

H. A. TODD.

LOUIS EMIL MENGER.
JUNE 29, 1871 — AUGUST 4, 1903.

IN MEMORIAM

A SAD accident has cut off the author of the present work from activity and effort before he could see the fruit of his years of earnest study. Since 1897 he had been collecting and digesting the bibliography of the Old French dialects, and during the winter of 1902 he decided to publish a section of the work he had in mind, that he might see whether the plan of the series met with approval, and might profit in the later parts by the criticisms of the first volume. This is no longer possible ; but could the author have foreseen the untimely ending of his life, he would no doubt have asked that the book still be judged with the calm, scientific spirit that knows and seeks nothing but truth ; and its appearing as a memorial volume implies in no wise a disposition to alter in this regard what would have been his wish.

The material for subsequent volumes in the *Manual of Old French Dialects*, projected by Dr. Menger, is limited to card references, and unfortunately is not in a form sufficiently advanced to be utilized for publication. An indication of the scope which might have been given to it is furnished by an article which appeared in *Modern Language Notes*, vol. XVIII, pp. 106–111.

Louis Emil Menger was born June 29, 1871, at Clinton, Mississippi. After graduating from Mississippi College, and teaching two years at Vicksburg, he entered the Johns Hopkins University. In the third year of his stay he was Fellow in Romance Languages, and in June, 1893, received the degree of Doctor of Philosophy. For a year he was Instructor, and for three years Associate at the Johns Hopkins; in 1897 he was appointed Associate Professor at Bryn Mawr College, and three years later was made Professor of Romance Philology and Italian. In December, 1900, he was married to Miss Elizabeth Buckley. During the summer of 1903 he travelled with his wife in Italy, and on August 4 was drowned while bathing in the Lago Maggiore at Ghiffa. A fuller sketch of his life with a list of the monographs and reviews he had published is given by his friend and colleague, Professor F. De Haan, in *Modern Language Notes*, vol. XVIII, pp. 225–226.

Dr. Menger's straightforward, manly character and his kindly disposition are familiar to all who were associated with him. He was an able teacher and a zealous investigator, but that which gave the greatest promise of a life of usefulness and success was the steadiness of development in his intelligence and knowledge. Thus Part I of the *Manual of Old French Dialects* is not a measure of the best he could have done, but an indication of the far greater attainment which might have been reached had not his life come to a sudden end just as he was approaching the period of full maturity and power.

E. C. A.

CONTENTS

ix

INTRODUCTION

I now offer the first part of a work, the advantages, difficulties, and necessary deficiencies of which students of Old French dialects will at once appreciate. We have, for the present, several grammars of Old French which are, doubtless, as good as they can be made at this time; additions to our knowledge of that subject must come, for the most part, from two sources: A more intimate acquaintance with the individual part that the separate Old French dialects played in the history of various phonological or morphological changes, and an observation of the bearing which modern dialects and sub-dialects have on the developments of the older language. Up to a comparatively few years ago we heard little of scientific investigation of the modern dialects. Then, almost suddenly, attention was diverted to them, and scholars, in their enthusiasm for this new study, neglected a most essential feature of work done by many minds, as was the work on the old dialects: They omitted a gathering of their results, the synthesis that follows analysis and that renders conclusions accessible to all. Certain it is that we have no one book to which the student may go whenShe wishes to learn, for example, what texts belong to a given dialect, the relative dates of originals and manuscripts, or even the exact titles of printed (and especially early) editions of the texts; nor is there a place whereShe may find the characteristics of the dialects succinctly stated, or a guide to the history and results of discussion on these characteristics.

A work of the nature just indicated is lacking, and in all these years no one has even promised to satisfy our needs in this regard. I therefore present now the first cast of the first book of reference on Old French dialects, in the hope that it may be of help to my colleagues who are specializing on other points, and to beginners who wish to learn something of Old French dialects but have no guide of the kind through the labyrinth of information which, up to this time, has been permitted to remain scattered. My work may be dubbed by some a mere "compilation," though scholars of intimate acquaintance with studies on dialects will, perchance, give me credit for little additions to our knowledge of that subject, interspersed here and there in the pages that follow. It were presumptuous in me to cite as my models some very noteworthy compilations, the constant companions of workers in Old French philology. Besides, does not a certain and even a large portion of original work consist in setting old facts in a new light? I intend that my compilation shall lend to each dialect as presented a definite setting; the student can derive from it definite ideas and information with regard to each dialect, its texts and peculiarities. If my work is the only one to which he may go for both general and detailed information, or else for references, on these points, it needs no apology for its existence.

I have reserved any discussion of the general questions of the origin, development, or boundaries of dialects until I shall have completed my treatment of the individual dialects. A satisfactory *résumé* of the points of the subject is to be found in an article by Horning.[1] To my mind, "Norman," "Picard," "Burgundian," "Lorraine," and the like, whatever else the terms may imply as names of dialects, will always be used to indicate given points, movable if you will, around which are to be grouped certain phenomena which are marked in those regions; the fact that these dialect districts are not to be bounded as speech regions as definitely as they are, or were, politically and geographically

[1] *Zt. Rom. Phil.* XVII, 160c–187 ; cf. *Romania*, XXII, 604–607.

does not lessen their value as *points d'appui* for the student. In that sense I shall use the names.

The reader of this book will probably wonder at times whether the work is meant as a grammatical treatise or as a collection of references — a bibliography. In a way it is meant as both. In the grammatical part I have tried to write, at greater or less length, on the more important points, so that the student who, presumably, has not been over the ground as I have, may know at once what these points are. In the bibliographical portions I have given the essential references I have found in the monographs, journals, and books that are in the average library of institutions where studies like the present are likely to be pursued. I have endeavored to select, in the first place, representative texts (and not all the texts) of the beginning, middle, and end of the centuries in which the given dialect literature may be said to have flourished (using the word "literature," of course, in a restricted sense); again, I have chosen those texts to be consulted in collections like, for example, the *Altfranzosische Bibliothek* or the *Anciens Textes Français*, or else those published in journals, especially in the *Romania* and the *Zeitschrift fur Romanische Philologie*;[1] my object has been to use those texts to which the student is most likely to have access. My book is intended, for the most part, as a guide to be in the hands of the student when he is working for himself on the points to which I refer. For example, I do not indicate the location of manuscripts further than to say they are of London or Paris, as it may be; I make only what I consider necessary remarks about some of the manuscripts. Any one wishing to look up any especial manuscript mentioned can easily find his way by following my references. I hope that these

[1] To which I shall usually refer as "*Rom.*" and "*Zt.*," for the sake of brevity. The third most commonly cited journal, the *Literaturblatt fur Germanische und Romanische Philologie*, I refer to as "*Ltblt.*"

and all other references will suggest sufficient information to put the right kind of a student on the right track for investigations of ~~his~~ ^{her} own.   When, in ~~his~~ ^{her} study of my work, such a student arrives at the stage whereShe can detect deficiencies in the work, I shall feel that my labor has not been in vain.

I begin with the Anglo-Norman dialect as being probably the most important for the general student of Old French philology.   This importance is derived from the following fact: The first half-dozen texts in our list offer us speech characteristics of an Old French dialect at a time for which manuscripts in the Île-de-France dialect are unknown. Many phenomena recorded in our early texts become, at a later date, part of the history of the Île-de-France speech. The study of the first appearances of such phenomena must, then, be of the greatest importance.

My order of treatment for each dialect will be the following: —

I. Any necessary general remarks on the given dialect as a whole, its especial significance, its difficulties, or any question of importance raised by students of the dialect.

II. Bibliography of the most important representative texts in the given dialect, and detailed information with regard to these texts.   This information will be comprised under the following headings, and always in the order here indicated: —

1. General notes on the text or its author.

2. The published edition used by me.

3. Notes on the manuscripts followed in these editions.

4. Date of the original composition of the text, or date of the manuscript on which the edition is based.[1]

5. References to detailed studies on the language of each text.

III. Phonology and morphology of the given dialect.

[1] It may sometimes be more convenient to give the date of the Ms. in connection with the remarks under § 3.

THE ANGLO–NORMAN DIALECT

THE ANGLO-NORMAN DIALECT

I. GENERAL CONSIDERATIONS

WHAT is Anglo-Norman? The name indicates that Anglo-Norman is the speech carried into England by the Normans and there so modified as to need a new name to distinguish it from Norman spoken on the continent. We must not suppose, however, that we have to do with an idiom which, brought over by the Norman colony, — transplanted on new soil, so to speak, — underwent a regular course of gradual growth followed by gradual decay; such was not the case. The one great distinguishing characteristic of Anglo-Norman is its irregularity.

To explain. The first question of the inquiring student will be: What was the influence of French on English, and what was the influence of English on French? Was the modification of the French language which took place on English territory due to the contact and the mutual influence of the two languages? The limited extent of the influence of any such contact on the French becomes evident when we note the very restricted progress that French made in England, and the consequent lack of probability of modifications arising from a defective use of French by the inhabitants of England. French never became the language of the populace; many facts indicate that it was employed mostly by the higher, perhaps to some degree by the middle classes, and there is no reason for supposing that it may not have been at least understood by people outside of those classes; writings like those of Bozon (first half of the fourteenth century, cf. p. 35) were surely not addressed to court circles. It was, nevertheless, essentially the language of the higher circles, and even among these its cultivation was not of long continuance. Toward the end of the thirteenth century we find that a knight, Gautier de Bibbysworth,[1] compiled an elementary treatise for the benefit of children of the aristocracy who might wish to learn French. This fact points toward English and not French as the mother tongue of the English aristocracy of the time. Toward the latter part of the fourteenth century French was not even taught regularly in the schools, nor to children of the nobles, nor used in court. At this time begin English translations of French originals, and Langland and Chaucer commence to write.

Furthermore, though this seems but natural, French did not impress itself except in those sections of England where Frenchmen actually settled. In more than one province it remained either entirely unintelligible or else little known. In any possibility of organic development the transplanted language evidently lacked, therefore, an indispensable element of organic growth, — becoming a part of the life of the great masses of the people; it had no new blood infused into it, so to speak, and was doomed to early decay. The first evidences of this decay took the form of simplification; such as, in phonology, the monophthongization of diphthongs; in morphology, the reduction of cases. Our Anglo-Norman writers had no vigorous living tongue to draw on; they were far removed from the mother French, and they were hearing English all about them. Thus it was that they forgot many niceties of speech observed on the continent, and thus it is that we find examples of simplifications in Anglo-Norman before we note them on the continent. (This explains, incidentally, why illustrations of developments in Anglo-Norman figure so largely in our Old French grammars.)

If, then, Anglo-Norman did not enjoy a regular organic development, our writers had no stable usage of the language

---

[1] Cf. *Rom.* XXXII, 44.

in England from which to draw; the only check on licenses they took with the idiom was, therefore, their greater or less acquaintance with French of the continent, and we must expect the usage of each writer to vary according to his knowledge of that French, and his communication with France. This personal equation, this independence of each individual author, goes far toward explaining irregularities in Anglo-Norman, and is typical of it. We need not be surprised to find a writer, even in the last days of Anglo-Norman, using French that is quite correct, like, for example, that found in the Bible translation spoken of on page 33. While it is most important to recognize the fact of variations in the language incidental to the varying degree of culture of each writer, we must not forget, either, that there do exist numbers of traits common to Anglo-Norman authors and scribes as a whole; in no case, however, do these traits represent stages of consistent development. They are but the decay, the simplification already referred to, illustrations of carelessness as to distinctions that were being observed on the continent. That most of these simplifications should later take place in French proper makes a study of the circumstances attendant upon their history in Anglo-Norman the more interesting. Such changes on the mainland were, as a rule, consequent upon the action of some general principle, and their regular course can be traced in texts of the continent. In Anglo-Norman the alterations were, for the most part, fortuitous; they are not necessarily general among the writers of any one epoch, and fixed time limits can hardly be assigned for them.

We have still another reason for irregularities in this dialect, though it is rather a further illustration of the one just referred to (individual prerogative in Anglo-Norman). We need not think that the term " Anglo-Norman " refers exclusively to the dialect of the province of Normandy as used in England. History indicates that men from many parts of France took part in the expedition of William the Conqueror.

Moreover, several phenomena may be cited in Anglo-Norman which are not to be found in Norman. It seems but natural to suppose, however, that the essential basis of the original French in England was Norman, and, for that matter, Norman influence had been at work in England twenty-four years before the advent of the Conqueror; that is, during the reign of Edward the Confessor. The preponderating political influence in England was that of Norman leaders, and the literary men of France most likely to be attracted to England were Norman men of letters, — friends, it may be, of the political chiefs. Any exclusive Norman influence must have waned, however, at least after the end of the twelfth century, since in 1204 the individuality of Normandy itself was merged into that of the Île-de-France; furthermore, during the reign of Henry III (1216–1272), who married Eleanor of Provence, the court colony received additions from the southern provinces of France. We may say then that "Anglo-Norman" seems to designate more aptly the early period of the dialect, while "Anglo-French," as used by some scholars, would better apply to the latter part of it; neither defines accurately the entire period.

We have now seen that our dialect underwent no progressive, organic development; the history of the language cannot be divided into successive stages, either according to dates or according to leading lines of growth; the dialect is, to a great extent, the product of the individual caprices of writers; it has not even a fitting name. The only general definition of Anglo-Norman possible is that it is bad French as used in England (during the Middle Ages); even at this point we have to modify our characterization by saying that it was often "bad" only as regards the date of its use, since what was "bad" French in Anglo-Norman territory, afterwards might become good French on the continent, where Anglo-Norman simplifications often became the rule.

I have already manifested my want of confidence in the feasibility of dividing Anglo-Norman phenomena into periods. Perhaps I should say something of the so-called "sub-dialects," supposed by some to exist within the Anglo-Norman. If what I have said with regard to the lack of any stable, organic principle of life in Anglo-Norman be true, surely little stress is to be laid upon any divisions of the language within that dialect. Indications of such divisions have been traced, at least between the north and the south, as based, for example, on the rhyming or not rhyming of u with $\ddot{u}$. It is almost an axiom that a language which is being learned by an individual, or collectively by a town, a province, or a nation, becomes modified in proportion to the difficulties of the learners in imitating the sounds of the new language they hear about them. Now if French made little headway among the masses of English-speaking people, variations in one of our texts as compared with another hardly arose from the greater or less ease with which the writer, or the people of the section from which the writer came, learned and spoke French. The average Anglo-Norman scribe represented only himself; he availed himself of French as a literary exercise in most cases, and the peculiarities in his text reflect mainly his individual caprice. From what sources, then, can we derive any justification for supposing sufficient cohesion or crystallization in any one section of the country to dignify that section with the appellation of a "sub-dialect"?[1]

[1] Bibliography on the foregoing pages, and general Anglo-Norman bibliography: The above ideas are derived from many sources, — notes jotted down in the course of much reading. I append a few references: —

For a general introduction to the study of Anglo-Norman, see Vising: *Étude sur le Dialecte Anglo-Normand du XIIe Siècle*, Upsala, 1882, pp 5–15; Behrens in Paul's *Grundriss der Germanischen Philologie*, I[1], 799 ss, and in *Französische Studien*, V, heft 2, Meyer in the introduction to the edition of Bozon (cf. below, p. 35), pp. lii–lvii.

For expressions concerning the effect of the influence of individual authors in Anglo-Norman, see Vising, *Étude*, pp. 13 and 14; Mall,

II. TEXTS

I have endeavored to arrange the texts, now to be enumerated, in chronological order. In doing this several methods occur to one. For example, we might adopt an arrangement according to the time in which the original was actually

Cumpoz (cf. below, p. 9), pp. 39, 40, and 63; *Romania*, I, 71; XII, 201; *Zt. Rom. Phil.* VI, 485; XXI, 575.

For the term "Anglo-French" and distinctions to be observed between Norman and general French influence in Anglo-Norman, see Suchier, *Français et Provençal*, p. 163; Gröber's *Grundriss*, I, 572; *Französ. Stud.* V, 2, 2; *Rom.* XXVIII, 151; *Krit. Jhrsbrcht. Fortschritte Rom. Phil.* II, 1, 248; Paul's *Grundriss*, I[1], 808.

Some notes on sub-dialects may be seen in Vising, *Étude*, pp. 11–12, and in *Ltblt. Germ. u. Rom. Phil.* IX, 176.

There are two further points to which reference should be made, detailed treatment of which is forbidden by the nature of my *Manual* as a whole. These points are the use of accent marks in Anglo-Norman manuscripts and peculiarities of Anglo-Norman versification. On the accents we have the monograph of K. Lincke : *Die Accente im Oxforder und im Cambridger Psalter sowie in anderen altfranzösischen Handschriften*, Erlangen, 1886. The following occasional references may be added: *Zt. Rom. Phil.* III, 161; X, 299; *Romania*, XII, 208, 434; Suchier, *Grammatik*, p. 8; Plåhn, *Quatre Livres des Reis* (full title below, p. 16), p. 5 (here are many useful references); Cloran, *Dialogues of Gregory* (see below, p. 21), p. 72. — For the study of Anglo-Norman versification the best starting-point is the review by P. Meyer (*Romania*, XV, 144), of a dissertation on the subject by Vising. Important remarks by Koschwitz and Mussafia are to be found in *Zt. Rom. Phil.* II, 339; III, 597.

The following books are almost indispensable in a study of Anglo-Norman, and I shall take it for granted that they are in the hands of every student using my work: Suchier, *Grammatik*, and *Vie de Seint Auban* (cf. below, p. 28); Stürzinger, *Orthographia Gallica* (*Altfranz. Bibl.* VIII), Heilbronn, 1884; Behrens (work just referred to); Stimming, *Boeve* (cf. below, p. 26). This last volume mentioned (*Boeve*) comes near combining most of the others cited. I hope I may facilitate the use of it for the beginner by the headings I have adopted in the treatment of my subject, and by the frequent references to Stimming.

composed. This time may be approximated in three ways:
First, from a consideration of the established facts as to
dates in the lives of the authors. But in the case of most
of our texts, even when the name of the author is known,
which is rarely the case, our biographical notices of him are
most meagre. Second, from internal evidence. Such evidence is obtainable, for the most part, only in works dealing
with historical or legendary material; in dealing with historical evidence we are too often thwarted by the inaccuracy of
historical allusions, and there exist few legends out of the
great mass of mediæval material, the date of whose appearance or episodes can be or have been accurately stated.
Third, from a study of the language. Here we have to distinguish between the language of the author and that of the
writer or copyist of the manuscript. (In only one Anglo-
Norman text are we sure that author and scribe were one
and the same person, viz., in that of Frère Angier; cf. p. 21.)
Such a distinction is possible to any important extent only
in poetical compositions, where the rhymes furnish a comparatively stable element; and even then deductions have
to be weighed most carefully (the prose text of the *Lois
de Guillaume* is one of the exceptions here; cf. p. 11). The
majority of our texts have not been studied with this especial point in view.

Or again, we may arrange our texts by following the dates
of the manuscripts at our command. These dates are
arrived at with fair accuracy by the science of paleography.
This science affords the only criteria that may be applied to
all our texts alike, because it follows in every case certain
definite and fixed principles of discrimination. The manuscript represents, as a rule, as far as anything we have can
represent it, the language used by the scribe and his con-
temporaries (though even at best the scribe's mode of representing the language will be modified by previous training
and tradition; by the character of the original or copy
which he is transcribing, and by other circumstances). In

the study of individual authors, it may be of prime importance to fix the date of the compositions of the author. But in an investigation such as the present, where we are concerned with dialects as a whole, we are more interested in the monuments of that dialect arranged so as to show the consecutive history of the language. I have, therefore, followed the order of the time of the manuscripts of my texts as nearly as I could. For the sake of consistency I have adopted this arrangement even when the date of the original composition is accurately known (in which cases I have indicated such dates as well as those of the manuscripts). As a matter of fact, the order of most of the earliest (and more important) texts would not be seriously affected by rearranging them according to the known or supposed dates of their original forms.

We must bear in mind with regard to all of our earlier texts, those, viz., of the middle and last part of the twelfth century, that for many reasons they might almost equally well be classed as Norman, — because of the comparatively slight variations in their forms as compared with those of Norman texts of the continent; because, in some cases, the author or copyist was born in Normandy; because the date of the original compositions fell so shortly after that of the Norman Conquest.

PHILIPPE DE THAÜN

1. Philippe is our first real Anglo-Norman author. He may be called so, however, only because his language begins to show traces of peculiarities which later became characteristic of Anglo-Norman (such as *ie*: *e*, *ǫ*: *ǫ*, and the loss of inflection). Otherwise he might be classed as Norman.[1]

[1] Cf. Mall, *Cumpoz*, pp. 19, 36, 40, 45, 68, 100; G. Paris, *Vie St. Gilles*, p. xv (full title below, p. 23); Gröber, *Grundriss*, II, 1, 483. For the few facts we have of Philippe's life, cf. Wright, *Biographia Britannica Literaria*. Anglo-Norman period, London, 1846, p. 86; Walberg, *Bestiaire*, p. xvii. Thaün (Taün, Thaon, Than) is near Caen, in Normandy.

CUMPOZ

2. *Li Cumpoz Philipe de Thaün,* herausgegeben von E. Mall, Strassburg, 1873. The introduction (111 pages) to this edition is one of the important early contributions to the general science of Old French philology, and remains a standard work to this day.

3. Mall used four principal manuscripts, all Anglo-Norman, besides notes on three others from the Vatican. These are all described at length (pp. 1–19). Mall follows the S[loane] Ms. of the beginning of the thirteenth century, when supported by one of the older Mss , of which the most authoritative is the imperfect A[rundel] Ms. of the twelfth century. The L[incoln] and the C[otton] Mss. are of about the middle of the twelfth century.

4. The *Cumpoz* is older than the *Bestiaire;* this becomes evident from a comparison of speech differences and from internal evidence; the *Cumpoz* was written before the end of February, 1120.[1] The year generally given is 1119

5. For the language see Mall's introduction. There is likewise a separate study (of 70 pages) by L. Fenge: *Sprachliche Untersuchung der Reime des Computus,* in Stengel's *Ausgaben und Abhandlungen,* LV, Marburg, 1886. This work comprises a Rimarium, a Grammar of the rhymes (pp. 18–34), and a Glossary of the *Cumpoz.*

BESTIAIRE

1, 2. *Le Bestiaire de Philippe de Thaün,* E. Walberg, Paris, 1900.[2]

3. For the Mss. add to the information in the edition the note referred to in *Romania,* XXXI, 175. Walberg

[1] Cf. Mall, pp. 20, 24; Walberg, *Bestiaire,* p. lxxx; G. Paris, *Lit. Fr. Moy. Age,* p. 246.

[2] Cf. the additional notes by Walberg in *Zt Rom. Phil.* XXV, 697 and the careful reviews of Paris, *Rom.* XXIX, 589 ; Herzog, *Zt.* XXVI, 248, and Tobler, *Herrig's Archiv,* CV, 194.

used as a basis the London Ms. of the second half of
the twelfth century, written in the same dialect as the
original.

4. The usual date assigned to this text is about 1130;
Walberg thinks it before, rather than after, that year.

5. For the language see Walberg's introduction.

ALEXIS

1. This text finds a place in our present bibliography in
so far as the two oldest Mss., and probably one other, were
written in England.[1]

2. *La Vie de Saint Alexis*, G. Paris et L. Pannier, Paris,
1872. This edition (together with Mall's *Cumpoz*, already
referred to) marks an epoch in the science of Old French
philology.

3. The Anglo-Norman Mss. are known as Mss. L and A.
The first is so designated from the Abbey of Lambspringen
to which it belonged originally. This Ms. has been edited
separately four different times, first by Mueller, in 1845.
Its date is the middle of the twelfth century.[2] Paris, in his
edition (pp. 171–176), gives a detailed collation of it. Ms.
A is of the Ashburnham collection, quite inferior to L, but
hardly any later. It suffered from a "corrector" of a little
later date than the copyist; the "corrector" tried to im-
prove A by such means as changing the assonances to
rhymes; to this end he sacrificed sense, grammar, and
metre, and often rendered his original unintelligible. Paris
gives variants from this Ms. at the foot of each page of his
text.[3] Ms. P, now in Paris, was probably written in Eng-

---

[1] The *Alexis* (meaning thereby the *Alexis* of the Anglo-Norman
Mss.) is often referred to as an Anglo-Norman text. Cf., for example,
Meyer-Lübke, *Gram. Lang. Rom.* II, 396; *Zt. Rom. Phil.* IV, 644;
Such. *Gram.* p. 5.

[2] Cf. Paris ed. pp. 2, 3, 28, and 137.

[3] Cf. the edition, pp. 2, 4, and 137.

land; it is of the latter part of the thirteenth century. Paris gives variants from this Ms. too.[1]

4. The date has already been referred to as the middle of the twelfth century.

5. I know of no separate study on the language of the Anglo-Norman Mss. alone.

LAWS OF WILLIAM THE CONQUEROR

1. This text forms one of a numerous collection of laws, charts, decisions, and the like, of the time of the French occupation of England. William probably had nothing to do with the compilation, but it was attributed to him for the sake of the authority of his name, as were others to Edward the Confessor or to Henry I.

2. The text has been edited a number of times, the first edition bearing the early date of 1623; the last edition is that of J. E. Matzke: *Lois de Guillaume le Conquérant en Français et en Latin.* Textes et Étude Critique, avec une préface historique par C. Bémont, Paris, 1899.[2] The Latin text referred to in the title (and printed in this edition in columns parallel to the French laws) is one that is proved by Matzke to have been copied from the French (though not from the French Ms. preserved to us).

3. The single extant Ms. of Holkham (Norfolk) was written about 1230 The other Mss. (at least six) were lost, but not before being utilized in editions previous to that of Matzke.

---

[1] Cf. p. 3. The exact text of the Mss L, A, and P is given in Foerster und Koschwitz, *Uebungsbuch,* second ed Leipzig, 1902. Paris himself gives this reference in his latest edition of the text of the *Alexis,* Paris, Bouillon, 1903, p. 8 Cf. *Rom.* XXXI, 401.

[2] In connection with this edition, the detailed review of Suchier, *Litbl Germ u Rom Phil.* XXII, 119, must be taken into account, also that of Paris, *Rom.* XXIX, 153. There is a searching study on the general subject of the *Lois* in *Arch Stud. Neu. Spr. u. Lit.* CVI, 113–138 (Liebermann). Cf. *ibid.* CVII, 134.

4. The state of the language in the Holkham Ms. is much at variance with what we might expect to find, judging from the date of the Ms. In fact, the phonology is in many cases more consistently representative of earliest Anglo-Norman than is that of the Psalters or Philippe even. For this reason I place this text in my earliest group. Matzke supposed the composition of the *Lois* to have been between 1150 and 1170. Paris and Suchier (in their reviews) favor an earlier date, the reign of Henry I (1100–1135).

5. Matzke studies at length the language of the text (pp. xli–lii), comparing it with that of the oldest Anglo-Norman monuments.

OXFORD PSALTER

1. This text shows some characteristic Anglo-Norman traits, though not to such an extent as does the Cambridge *Psalter*.[1]

2. The first and only complete edition is that of Francisque Michel: *Libri Psalmorum Versio Antiqua Gallica,* Oxonii, 1860, 376 pp.

3. The Ms. used as a basis by Michel was that in the Bodleian Library; hence the name, "Oxford" *Psalter.* Since it is probable that the Oxford Ms. was written in the "Monasterii Montisburgi" (that is, Montebourg in Normandy), the name "Montebourg" *Psalter* is really more appropriate than the time-honored "Oxford" *Psalter.*[2] The date of this Ms. is toward the end of the twelfth century.[3]

4. As for the date of the original we may say only that the *Psalter* was probably translated in the course of the first half of the twelfth century, and that it is certainly

---

[1] Cf. *Zt. Rom. Phil.* I, 569. Much interesting and valuable information on Anglo-Norman versions of various parts of the Bible is given by Berger in his *Bible Française au Moyen Age*, Paris, 1884. See Meyer's review of the same, *Rom.* XVII, 121, and cf. Grober, *Grundriss*, II, 1, 484.

[2] Cf. *Zt.* I, 569; *Rom.* IX, 626.   [3] Such. *Gram.* p. 4.

older than the Cambridge *Psalter*, as is shown by certain peculiarities of its language; for example, medial *e* is not dropped, *l* does not vocalize, the III declension nouns *ber*, *jugierre*, etc., do not take *s* in the nominative, -ABAT and -EBAT endings are kept distinct, — the opposite of the state of affairs for all these points in the Cambridge *Psalter*.[1]

5. On the phonology of the Oxford *Psalter* we have the work of F. Harseim, *Vokalismus und Consonantismus im Oxforder Psalter, Romanische Studien*, IV, 273–327, — a somewhat diffuse and unequally proportioned article, though easy to refer to on account of its many subdivisions [2] For the morphology, there is the work of J. H. Meister, *Die Flexion im Oxforder Psalter*, Halle, 1877, 121 pp., which is to be controlled by the lengthy review, amounting to a new article, of Koschwitz in *Zt. Rom. Phil.* II, 480–489. A useful portion of Meister's work consists of his three pages of corrections (118–121) of Michel's text, the result of his own collation of the Oxford Ms.

CAMBRIDGE PSALTER

1. The evident Anglo-Norman provenance of this text has already been referred to (p 12) The study of speech differences within the text shows that the *Psalter*, as we have it, is the work of three different copyists or translators The first part, psalms I to CXXIV, is the only one that may be attributed to the old translator of the *Versio Hebraica*. From CXXIV to CXXXI there is a break. The second part, CXXXI to CXLVIII, had as its translator the copyist of the first part. The third part, Canticles, etc., is from a translation of the Gallican *Psalter*.[3] That the Oxford and

---

[1] *Zt.* I, 569–570.   [2] Cf. *Zt. Rom. Phil* IV, 464.

[3] This is the summary of Schumann's results (cf *Litblt.* V, 392), though the idea of such divisions was not original with Schumann He gives a detailed history of the subject on the first page of his article (for title see above, § 5).

Cambridge psalters are not the work of the same translator has been definitely proved.[1]

2. The edition is again one of F. Michel: *Le Livre des Psaumes*, Paris, 1876.[2]

3. The relations of the two Mss., the Cambridge and the Paris, are discussed by Schumann (pp. 4–6). The Ms. at Cambridge represents the labor of the copyist, Eadwin of Canterbury, and for this reason the collection is at times spoken of as "Eadwin's *Psalter*," again as the "Canterbury *Psalter*." The Paris Ms. is later than the Cambridge and often shows more correct readings; both copyists doubtless had the original before them.

4. Our text is older than the *Quatre Livres des Rois*, and probably falls in the reign of Henry II (1154–1189).[3] The date usually assigned is about 1160.

5. On the phonology we have W. Schumann: *Vokalismus und Konsonantismus des Cambridger Psalters*, Heilbronn, 1883 (*Franzos. Studien*, IV, 4), 69 pp. — an excellent work.[4] On the morphology we have E. Fichte: *Die Flexion im Cambridger Psalter*, Halle, 1879, 96 pp. This is to be controlled by the lengthy revision of it by Schumann at the end of the latter's work just noted (pp. 51–69).

ARUNDEL PSALTER

1. This *Psalter* may be so called from the name of the Ms. (Arundel, 230) in which it is found in the British Museum. It is the only known interlinear version of the Gallican *Psalter* and is peculiar in that the French words are placed above the corresponding Latin ones without any regard to the proper order of the French sentence. It may

---

[1] Cf. *Zt.* XI, 513.   [2] Cf. *Zt.* I, 568, for review.

[3] Cf. Paris, *Vie St. Gilles*, p. xxii; Such. *Gram.* p. 5; *Zt.* I, 569.

[4] Cf. *Rom.* XVI, 608; *Litblt.* V, 392. There is a dissertation by K. Dreyer: *Der Lautstand im Camb. Psalt.*, Greifswald, 1882, which I have not seen.

represent the original form of the Gallican *Psalter;* [1] it is truer to the Latin than is the Oxford *Psalter.*

2. Only the first 53 psalms of this Ms. have been published up to the present, — these by Beyer, in *Zt. Rom. Phil.* XI, 513–534; XII, 1–56.

3. The Ms spoken of above is the only one mentioned.

4. The Ms. is of the twelfth century, and that is as definite a date as we may assign for the present.

5. No study of the language has been published. [2]

QUATRE LIVRES DES ROIS

1. As long as the edition mentioned below remains the only one, we seem to be justified in placing this text in our list, though its Anglo-Norman provenance has been called into question. [3]

2. The edition referred to is that of Le Roux de Lincy. *Les Quatre Livres des Rois,* Paris, 1841. In consulting this text one should note the revision of it by Ollerich at the end of Schlosser's dissertation (mentioned below). This revision has the following basis: on the Ms. of the *Rois* are written many corrections of the main body of the text; the corrections were used inconsistently and indiscriminately by De Lincy. Ollerich studied and divided them into four sets. [4] The first set was made by the copyist of the Ms. The

---

[1] Cf. *Jhrsbrcht. Rom Phil.* I, 375.

[2] I have inserted a number of examples from this text (in my phonology and morphology of Anglo-Norman), some of which are very interesting; great stress is not to be laid on them, however, until the Ms. shall have been made the subject of further study To judge from the printed edition, a number of peculiarities in the Ms may be due to a very indifferent scribe. [A complete edition of the *Psalter* is now being prepared.]

[3] Cf. *Zt.* I, 569; *Rom* VII, 346, XV, 641, Meyer-Lubke, *Gram. Lang. Rom* I, 190, 196

[4] He calls these "Correcturen der ersten Hand," "Correcturen der zweiten Hand," "Correcturen der jungeren Hand," and "Correcturen der modernen Hand."

second may have been so too; in any case it is old enough to be taken into account; the others are worthless for a study of the language.

3. De Lincy's edition rests on the only Ms. known for a long time, the Mazarine, of the second half of the twelfth century, undoubtedly by an Anglo-Norman scribe; but Berger and Meyer have directed attention to other Mss., and the original of the text may be continental and not Anglo-Norman.[1]

4. The *Rois* is to be placed a little later than the Cambridge *Psalter*, probably about 1170.[2]

5. For the phonology we have P. Schlosser: *Die Lautverhältnisse der Q. L. R.*, Bonn, 1886 (dissertation); also the first few pages of a work concerned with the general morphology of the *Rois*: R. Plähn, *Les Quatre Livres des Reis*, Gottingen, 1888 (diss.). For the verbs alone we have K. Merwart, *Die Verbalflexion in den Q. L. R.*, Wien, 1880, 19 pp. Schlosser's work is based on Ollerich's corrections (referred to above); Merwart's has the advantage of giving the actual count of all phenomena treated. I have not seen a dissertation by W. Bartels: *Wortstellung in den Q. L. R.*, Hannover, 1886.

ROLAND

1. This text, like the *Alexis*, may be included in our bibliography; the relatively best Ms. of it is an Anglo-Norman one.

2. The standard edition of the Ms. is that of Stengel: *Das Altfranzösische Rolandslied*, Heilbronn, 1878. This edition was especially valuable because it was a diplomatic one, and because accompanying it was a photographic reproduction of the entire Ms. (published separately from the

---

[1] Cf *Rom.* XVII, 125, XXV, 186; G. Paris, *La Littérature Normande avant l'Annexion*, Paris, 1899, p. 36, f.-n. 3.

[2] Cf. *Zt.* I, 569; Schlösser, *o.c.* p. 4, f.-n. 1; Such. *Reimpredigt* (*Bibl Norman.* 1), p xviii, 13.

text, however). Stengel's work on this edition is now practically incorporated in his new critical edition of the *Roland* (Vol. I, Leipzig, 1900), the basis of which remains the Oxford Ms.

3. The Ms. was adequately described, for the first time, by Stengel in the introduction to the edition of 1878.

4. The date of the Oxford Ms. is about 1170.

5. We have no separate study on the subject of the general Anglo-Norman characteristics of the Ms. References for works on the language of the *Roland* are given by Seelmann in his *Bibliographie des Altfranz. Rolandsliede,* Heilbronn, 1888, p. 59 *ss.*

BRANDAN

1. The Anglo-Norman version of the legend of St. Brandan is the oldest one known in a vulgar speech of the Middle Ages.[1]

2. The poem was published by Suchier, in *Romanische Studien*, I (1875), 553–588, under the title "Brandan's Seefahrt."

3. This edition was based on the London Ms., Cotton Vesp., of the end of the twelfth century. It and other Mss. are commented on by Suchier in his Introduction.[2]

4. Internal evidence shows that the date of the original composition was 1121.[3]

5. For the study of the language we have to note several works; for the phonology, that of Vising, *Étude,* pp. 67–91, and of Hammer, *Zt. Rom. Phil.* IX, 75–115; for the

---

[1] Cf. Such. ed. pp. 553 and 555 ; Gröber, *Grundriss*, II, 1, 479.

[2] Details as to Mss. and editions are given by Vising, *Étude,* pp. 18–24. There is another work on the Mss. of the Brandan which I have not seen ; namely, that of M. Wien: *D. Verhältniss d. Hss. d. anglonormann. Brandanlegende,* Halle, 1886.

[3] Such. ed. p. 553; Vising, *Étude,* p. 24. Mall always spoke of the *Brandan* as contemporaneous with the *Cumpoz* (cf. pp. 80 and 82). See a note by Walberg, *Bestiaire,* p. lxxxi, f.-n., and cf. *Rom.* XXIX, 590, f.-n. 1.

c

morphology that of Vising, *Étude*, pp. 96–100, and of Brekke, *Étude sur la Flexion dans le Voyage de Saint Brandan*, Paris, 1884, 77 pp. The last few pages of Hammer's article are devoted to morphology, and Brekke treats the phonology incidentally. Neither one of these two seems entirely authoritative; Hammer's effort is satisfactory in its treatment of versification, but otherwise is not so good as that of Brekke. Many of the ideas of the latter are disputed in the reviews, which must be taken account of.[1] A résumé of the marked linguistic traits of the Brandan is given by Walberg in his *Bestiaire*, p. lxxxi. I have not seen a work by R. Birkenhoff: *Ueber Metrum u. Reim d. altfranz. Brandan*, Marburg, 1884.

GAIMAR

1. "Geoffrey Gaimar was a distinguished trouvère of the reign of Stephen (1135–1154). . . . He was the first who published an Anglo-Norman version of the history of the British kings by Geoffrey of Monmouth."[2]

2. "*Lestorie des Engles solum la translacion Maistre Geffrei Gaimar.*" Edited by Hardy and Martin. Two volumes, liii + 404 and xlii + 294. London, 1888 (in *Rerum Britannicarum Medii Aevi Scriptores*). This edition has been unfavorably reviewed.[3]

3. A discussion of the four Mss. of the *Estorie* is given by Vising, *Étude*, pp. 25–28. He here criticises the study of the Mss. by Kupferschmidt.

4. The date of the composition of the *Estorie* has been

[1] Cf. *Rom.* XV, 628; *Zt.* IX, 158; *Litbtl.* VI, 370.

[2] Wright, *Biogr. Brit. Lit.*, pp. 151–154, speaks of Gaimar. Cf. Meyer-Lubke, *Gram.* I, 561; *Litbtl.* IV, 311; *Roman. Stud.* IV, 417. The portion of Gaimar's history taken from Geoffrey of Monmouth is lost. Cf. also Grober, *Grundriss*, II, 472.

[3] Cf. Meyer in *Rom.* XVIII, 314–318. In this review, as well as in Vising, *Étude*, p. 25, will be found references to other editions of the *Estorie*, in whole or in part.

established, from internal evidence, as falling between 1145 and 1151.[1]

5 On the language the most careful work is that of Vising, *Étude*, pp. 80–91, for phonology; pp. 100–103 for morphology. Kupferschmidt, in the course of an investigation[2] into the relations of the lay of Havelok with Gaimar's chronicle, gives seven pages (417–423) of remarks on Gaimar's language and versification.

ADGAR

1 All we know of this poet is the little that remains of what he tells us; and the first part of the Ms. containing his work, the part in which the mediæval poet generally introduces himself, is lost.   His name is Adgar, though, he says, most people call him " Willame."   Wright[3] calls him " William the Trouvère."   The legends he relates are not original with him, but translated from a Latin book which he says he took from the library of St. Paul's, London [4]

2. The complete edition of his works is that of C. Neuhaus: *Adgar's Marienlegenden*, Heilbronn, 1886 (*Altfranzosische Bibliothek*, IX).   Adgar's legend of Theophile (1080 lines) had already been published in *Zeit Rom. Phil.* I, 531–540, but, apparently, rather carelessly.[5]

3. The legends are preserved in a London Ms. fully described by Neuhaus in his introduction.

4. The date of this Ms. is either the end of the twelfth or beginning of the thirteenth century.   Rolfs (see below), from a comparison of the language of Gaimar, Fantosme, and Adgar, judged that Adgar was nearer Gaimar, that is, about 1150.

---

[1] Cf. Wright, *o.c.* p. 154 (Wright specifies between 1147 and 1151) ; Vising, *Étude*, p. 33 , *Rom.* XVIII, 314

[2] *Roman Stud.* IV, 411–430 ; cf. *Rom.* IX, 480.

[3] *Biogr Brit Lit* p. 464.

[4] On Adgar, cf Grober, *Grundriss*, II, 1, 650.

[5] Cf. *Zt.* II, 81 ; *Rom.* VII, 343.

5. Neuhaus makes no study of the language in his edition, since that had already been done quite thoroughly by W. Rolfs in *Romanische Studien*, I, 179–236.[1]

FANTOSME

1. Jordan Fantosme is mentioned in several places, so that we are sure of a few facts of his life; he was a master in the schools at Winchester, and was present in the north of England when that district was invaded by the Scots under William the Lion in 1173 and 1174. It was this invasion which he afterward described in an Anglo-Norman *Chronique* in verse.[2]

2. The *Chronique* was published by F. Michel, as an appendix (pp. 531–613) to Vol. III of the *Chronique des Ducs de Normandie*, Paris, 1844. This was the second time that Michel published the poem, the first being in 1839 for the Surtees Society of Durham.[3] The next edition was that by Howlett[4] (Rolls Series, 1886). A new edition by Barbier is announced in *Rom.* XXX, 468.

3. The two Mss. of the *Chronique*, one of Durham and one of Lincoln, both of the thirteenth century, are described and compared by Vising.[5]

4. The date is determined, from internal evidence, to have been between 1174 and 1183.[6]

5. For Fantosme's language we have to refer to Vising's *Étude*, pp. 91–95 for the phonology, pp. 103–104 for the morphology.[7]

[1] See review by Vising, *Litblt.* IV, 180.

[2] Wright, *Biogr. Brit. Lit.* p. 221. Cf. Grober, *Grundriss*, II, 1, 638 (in the *Register*, p. 1270, this reference is incorrectly given as 636). [3] Cf. *Chron.* III, 613.

[4] Not Haslitt, as cited in *Litblt.* XIII, 416. [5] *Étude*, pp. 34–38.

[6] Cf. Vising, *Étude*, pp. 41, 42 ; *Litblt.* III, 17, IV, 311.

[7] On the metre of the *Chronique* there is a dissertation by H. Rose in *Roman. Stud.* V, 2, 301–382 (cf. *Litblt.* III, 352).

ANGIER

1. In the translation from Latin into Anglo-Norman of the Life and of the Dialogues of Gregory the Great we have one of the most valuable aids to the study of our dialect; this is because the translator gives his name, then the place and time of the manuscript, which he writes himself, and he shows care and correctness rarely to be found among Anglo-Norman scribes. We owe our knowledge of the work of this translator — a certain Frère Angier of Sainte Frideswide — to P. Meyer, who was the first ever to mention him.

2. Meyer edited 242 verses of the *Dialogues* in his *Recueil*, pp. 340–343. Later, in *Rom.* XII, 145–208, he published the *Vie de Saint Grégoire le Grand* in full (2954 lines) with notes on the Ms, author, and language, and a vocabulary. Selections consisting of the Prologues of the *Dialogues*, a prayer to the Holy Spirit and to the Trinity are given on pages 5–30 of the Dissertation of Timothy Cloran: *The Dialogues of Gregory the Great*, Strassburg, 1901.[1] Cloran promises a complete edition of the *Dialogues*, which are much longer then the *Vita*, since they contain 19,367 verses.

3, 4. The Ms. containing Angier's translations is in the Bibliothèque Nationale, Paris. Meyer, while not perfectly sure, considers it probable, and gives good reasons for his opinion, that we have in this Ms. Angier's autograph copy. Meyer's idea is that Angier first made a sketch ("brouillon," "minute") of his translation of the *Dialogues*, then copied them in full and dated them November 29, 1212. About a year and a half later he added the *Vie*, which he finished April 30, 1214. There is no paleographic argument against attributing the Ms. to these years; the writing is that of the first half of the thirteenth century.

5. Meyer gives an extended study of the phonology and

----

[1] For corrections of details in Cloran's work see *Rom.* XXXI, 174, *Mod. Lang. Notes*, XVI, 241 (Sheldon).

morphology of the *Vie* in his edition, pp. 193–201. Cloran studies the same in the *Dialogues*, pp. 40–53, following Meyer in the main, though giving some supplementary details (cf. also p. 4).

CHARDRI

1. About all we know of this poet is his name, and also that he lived in England. The three poems of his which we have are of some literary importance on account of the legends which they embody.[1] The *Petit Plet* is particularly interesting.[2]

2. John Koch, *Chardry's Josaphaz, Set Dormanz und Petit Plet*, Heilbronn, 1879 (*Altfranz. Bibl.* I). This edition was much criticised by Suchier[3] and Mussafia,[4] and is hardly what might be termed a definitive edition. Koch spells the name " Chardry," which is against the authority of the Mss.

3. The Mss. are three, the oldest in the British Museum and of the first half of the thirteenth century; this one served as the basis of Koch's text; the second Ms. is in Oxford, and of the middle or else second half of the thirteenth century; the third is in the Vatican and probably the work of two scribes, of the thirteenth and fourteenth centuries. The first two Mss. mentioned contain all three poems, the last only the *Petit Plet*.

4. Since the London Ms. was written before 1216, the original must have been composed in the course of the twelfth century.[5]

5. The language is studied by Koch, pp. xxv–xl, and these pages are carefully examined by Mussafia in his review.[6]

---

[1] In addition to Koch's study of these, there is a dissertation by A. Reinbrecht, *Die Legende von den sieben Schlafern und der Anglo-Normannische Dichter Chardri*, Gottingen, 1880. Cf. Koch, *Litblt.* II, 290 ; Such. *ib* 363, and Varnhagen, *Zt.* V, 162. One chapter of Reinbrecht's dissertation is devoted to the biography of Chardri, but offers nothing new. Cf. also Grober, *Grundriss*, II, 1, 643, 690.

[2] Cf. *Rom.* IX, 171.   [3] *Litblt.* II, 359.   [4] *Zt.* III, 591.
[5] Cf. Koch, *l.c.* XLVI; Suchier, *l.c.* p. 361.   [6] pp. 592–597.

GUILLAUME DE BERNEVILLE

1. A commune of the Manche bears the name of Berneville, and a text of the thirteenth century presents the name under the Latin form Bernevilla. The family of our poet probably moved from there to England, as did that of Philippe from Than. Certain contrarieties in the language of Guillaume are to be reconciled only when we consider him an Anglo-Norman and not a continental Norman. His language is superior to that of Fantosme, for example, and he holds honorable rank beside Philippe, Gaimar, or the author of the *Brandan*.[1]

2. *La Vie de Saint Gilles, par Guillaume de Berneville,* poème publié par G. Paris et A. Bos, Paris, 1881 (*Sociéte des Anciens Textes Français*)[2]

3. The one Ms. of the poem is that of the Laurentian library in Florence; it was, without any doubt, written in England, because it shows all the characteristics of Anglo-Norman writing of the thirteenth century.[3]

4. The date of this Ms. is the first half of the thirteenth century.[4] The original is older: from evidence based on the use of the names of the three Magi (Melchior, Gaspar, and Balthasar), which were not introduced into the West till after the pretended discovery of their bodies in Milan in 1158, we cannot date the original earlier than about 1170. The study of the grammatical forms, too, shows that the *Vie* was written after 1150.[5]

5. The language is studied at length, pp. xxvii–xxxiv; the contrariety already referred to is considered, pp. xvii–xxi. It consists in the fact that the style and the phonetics (with the exception of one trait, the fall of pretonic

---

[1] Cf. the edition, pp xv, xxi, and xxxv; Meyer-Lubke, *Gram.* I, 561; Grober, *Grundriss*, II, 1, 642.

[2] In the use of this text account should be taken of the important corrections of Introduction, Text, and Glossary by Mussafia, *Rom* XI, 594–598. [3] Ed. p. xvii. [4] Ed. p. xiv. [5] Ed. pp. xxv and xxvii.

e in hiatus: *jeu > ju*) are archaic, while the declension approaches very nearly the later Anglo-Norman inflection.

MODWENNE

1, 2. Suchier published 112 verses of the life of St. Modwenne in his *Vie de St. Auban*, pp. 54–58. It was taken from a Latin original of the first half of the twelfth century, for the lack of a manuscript copy of which Suchier postponed the complete edition of the Anglo-Norman poem.

3. The verses occur in an Oxford Ms.

4. The date of the Ms. is the first half of the thirteenth century.[1]

5. Suchier cites examples from this text in his *Auban*, but there is no detailed study of the forms.

ST. THOMAS

1. The long conflict between Thomas Becket and Henry II, and, more particularly, Becket's assassination and consequent repute as a martyr, furnished material for many "Vies" of the latter, both in Latin and in French. The oldest, and most important, French life of Thomas is that of Garnier de Pont Sainte-Maxence, composed between 1174 and 1176. Of this "Life" there are six Mss., all executed in England; it has been published twice,—by Bekker, in 1838, and by Hippeau, in 1859. A second life of Thomas is by a certain frère Benet, of probably the first quarter of the thirteenth century,[2] of which several Mss. exist. This is the biography published by F. Michel in his *Chronique des Ducs de Normandie*, III, 461–509 (same volume as that containing the *Chronique* of Fantosme).

---

[1] Cf. *Auban*, pp. 4 and 33, and the general remarks in Grober, *Grundriss*, II, 1, 647.

[2] According to Meyer, *St. Thomas*, p. ii, from whom all the above information is derived. Paris (*Vie St. Gilles*, p. xxii) gives the date as about 1172. Cf. also Grober, *Grundriss*, II, 1, 645.

Michel used a Ms. (and a poor one) of the Bibliothèque Nationale, and gives (pp. 615–630) variants from a British Museum Ms.

2. The edition of a life of Thomas most useful for our purposes is a third one, as given in the volume of P. Meyer: *Fragments d'une Vie de Saint Thomas de Cantorbéry*, Paris, 1885 (*Soc. Anc. Textes Fr.*).

3. These fragments are from a Ms in Courtrai consisting of four leaves; on each side of each leaf is a miniature and a fragment (all photographed and printed in the edition).

4. The writing of the Ms. indicates that it is of a date not later than the middle of the thirteenth century. The original may be placed between 1198 and the time of the Ms., it may be the year 1220. The author is unknown.[1]

5. Meyer mentions (pp. xxviii–xxxi) the characteristics of the text, dwelling particularly upon the point of the elision of *e* before a vowel.

ADAM

1. This is a very important text in connection with the history of the Mystères.[2]

2. Karl Grass: *Das Adamsspiel*, Halle, 1891 (*Romanische Bibliothek*, VI). This edition called forth several important reviews.[3] The text had already been published twice. Grass edits, as an appendix (p. 53), the "*Quinze Signes*" (360 lines), which follow directly upon the *Adam* in the Ms., but really have no connection otherwise with it, and do not belong to the Anglo-Norman dialect.[4]

3, 4. The single Ms., that of Tours, gave rise to a discussion as to whether or not it was written at two different epochs. Forster holds to this idea. He even assigns the

---

[1] Meyer ed. pp. iii, v, and xxvii.

[2] Cf Grober, *Grundriss*, II, 1, 712.

[3] Notably those of Tobler, *Litblt.* XII, 341 ; Such *Götting. Gelehrt. Anzeig* 1891, p. 685, and Mussafia, *Zeit. Oestr. Gymn* XLVI, 67.

[4] Cf *Rom.* XXI, 280, and *Jhrsbrcht. Rom Phil.* II, 1, 250.

first part, that in which our poem occurs, to the twelfth century.[1] This idea is not universally accepted, and the middle of the thirteenth century seems a safer date.

5. Grass offers a long study (pp. 111–142) of the language of the poem, comparing it with that of the Oxford and Cambridge *Psalters* and the *Quatre Livres des Rois.* Care must be exercised in consulting these pages, since, curiously enough, Grass apparently takes no notice of the ten pages (69–78) of Förster's corrections of his readings.

BEVIS OF HAMPTON

1, 2. *Der Anglonormannische Boeve de Haumtone,* zum ersten male herausgegeben von Albert Stimming, Halle, 1899 (*Bibliotheca Normannica,* VII). Suchier says (p. cxcv of the Introduction) that this edition is made with a "Grundlichkeit" and "Sachkenntniss" not to be noted in any other Anglo-Norman text.

3. The Mss., fully described by Stimming, pp. iii–viii, are two, both in Paris, one of the thirteenth and one of the fourteenth century.

4. The time of the original composition, if we judge from the state of the language, must have been the first half of the thirteenth century.[2]

5. The language is treated in the Introduction (pp. viii–xxxii) and again in the Appendix (pp. 171–240). The Appendix is a mine of information on Anglo-Norman phonology in general.

AMADAS AND YDOINE

1. The poem of this subject was very popular in England,[3] and the primitive form of it is the Anglo-Norman redaction.[4]

---

[1] A description of this Ms. had already been given, *Rom.* II, 91–95. Delisle here says he does not think the Ms. is to be placed before the middle of the thirteenth century.

[2] For general remarks on *Boeve,* cf. Gröber, *Grundriss,* II, 1, 572.

[3] Cf. *Rom.* XVIII, 627, f.-n.   [4] Cf. *Rom.* XXX, 633.

2. Andresen edited two fragments of the poem, the one of 140, the other of 146 lines, in *Zt. Rom. Phil.* XIII, 84–97.

3. These fragments he found on two pages of Ms. in the Gottingen library. There is another Ms. (Picard ?) in Paris, of the date 1288, edited by Hippeau · *Amadas et Ydoine, Poème d'Aventures*, Paris, 1863. (This edition I have not seen.)

4. Andresen supposes his Ms. to be of the first half of the thirteenth century [1] Meyer, in his review,[2] questions so early a date, but goes into no detail to disprove it

5. The editor makes a note (pp. 85–87) of the Anglo-Norman peculiarities of his text.

CHEVALIER, DAME ET CLERC

1, 2. This *fabliau*, of 586 verses, was edited by Meyer in *Rom.* I, 69–87, under the title " *Romanz de un Chivaler et de sa Dame e de un Clerk* "

3, 4. The Ms. is in Cambridge and was written in England toward the middle of the thirteenth century.

5. There is no detailed study of the language.

ST. AUBAN

1. The poem of this name treats of the life of the first martyr in England; in his honor the abbey of St. Auban was named, and there, in the thirteenth century many Mss were written; our present one, along with others, has been attributed to Matthew Paris, a celebrity of the abbey (died 1259). The editor of the poem (Atkinson) was of this opinion, doubtless an incorrect one.[3]

2. The first edition of the poem was that of R. Atkinson, *Vie de Seint Auban*, London, 1876 Many emendations of his text were made by reviewers.[4]

[1] Cf. *Zt.* XXI, 576   [2] *Rom* XVIII, 626

[3] Cf. Suchier, *Auban*, pp. 2 and 3 , Meyer, *Rom.* XV, 146 ; Gröber, *Grundriss*, II, 1, 617.

[4] A list of these reviews is given by Uhlemann, *Roman. Stud.* IV, 623.

3, 4. The Ms. is in Trinity College, Dublin, and of the middle of the thirteenth century. The original is of about the same date.[1]

5. On the language of the poem we have two works. First, the very important one of Suchier: *Ueber die Matthaeus Paris zugeschriebene Vie de Seint Auban*, Halle, 1876. This little volume developed out of what Suchier intended to be a review of Atkinson's edition. It deals with the authorship of the *Auban*, Anglo-Norman versification,[2] and some difficult points of Anglo-Norman phonetics. The other work is the rather prolix one of Uhlemann: *Ueber die Vie de Seint Auban in Bezug auf Quelle, Lautverhältnisse und Flexion*, in *Roman. Stud.* IV, 543–626.[3]

SARDENAI

1, 2. This little poem of 452 lines was published by G. Raynaud in *Rom.* XI, 531–537, under the title [Le Miracle de Sain]te Marie de Sard[enai].

3. There are four Mss. of the poem. The one from which Raynaud published his text was of Tours, the same as that containing the *Mystère d'Adam*.[4] Raynaud thought that the original poem was Picard, though the scribe had evidently had access to a model executed in England; later, our editor made the acquaintance of two other Mss. (of London and Oxford), which were by Anglo-Norman scribes, and in *Rom.* XIV, 88–93, he adds variant readings from these two Mss. Later still (*Rom.* XV, 354) Meyer describes a Ms. of Cambridge containing the *Miracle* and expresses

---

[1] Cf. *Rom.* V, 384.

[2] On this point, cf. the remarks of Meyer in *Rom.* XV, 146.

[3] Cf. the reviews in *Zt.* VI, 485 , *Litblt.* III, 15.

[4] Cf. p. 25. Grass, p. vi, mentions the *Miracle* in enumerating the contents of this Ms. ; but speaks of it as inedited, although Vol. XI of the *Romania* was in existence nine years before the date of Grass's publication.

his assurance that England was the original place of the composition.[1]

4. The date of the Tours Ms. is given as the middle of the thirteenth century;[2] that of London, the thirteenth;[3] that of Oxford the beginning of the fourteenth;[3] the date of the Cambridge Ms. is not mentioned.

5. Raynaud makes a few remarks on the language in *Rom.* XI, 530, and XIV, 87.

ASPREMONT

1. Many manuscripts of this important *chanson de geste* were written in England. In fact, the only complete manuscripts of it seem to have been executed either in England or in Italy.[4]

2. The text we refer to here is that edited by Langlois in *Rom.* XII, 446–458 (preceded by a fragment of *Otinel* from the same Ms.). The continuation of this *Aspremont* is given by Meyer, *Rom.* XIX, 205–216.

3. The Ms. used by Langlois is of the Bibliothèque Nationale, though originally from the archives of Lozère. Curiously enough, the fragment edited by Meyer, and now in Clermont, formerly belonged to and was a part of the Lozère Ms.[5]

4. The date of this Ms. is about the middle of the thirteenth century.[6]

---

[1] Raynaud, *Rom.* XIV, 87, corrects his own mistake with regard to *li eule* being Picard. (He had supposed that *eule* was feminine.) There are, however, several phenomena to be noted in the Tours Ms. he published which are not usually associated with Anglo-Norman, and which may be with Picard. For example, we may cite *viaut* (*volet*) 308, *dou peuple*, 21, *do Temple*, 363. The Oxford Ms. shows *volt*, but neither it nor the London Ms. offers a variant for the *dou* The Tours Ms. has *iaus* (*oculum*) constantly where the London and Oxford Mss. present *oilz*.   [2] *Rom* XI, 519.   [3] *Rom.* XIV, 82

[4] *Rom.* XIX, 201; here a list of the Mss. is given by Meyer; of these, five were from England.   [5] *Rom.* XIX, 204.

[6] *Rom.* XII, 434, and XIX, 203. [There are two foot-notes numbered "3" on this page.]

5. Langlois calls attention (p. 434) to a few peculiarities of the language and orthography, particularly the use of accent marks in the Ms.

MADELEINE

1. This little fragment of seventy-eight lines has an interesting bit of literary history connected with it; it was announced by its first editor, Kauffer, to be a composition of Richard the Lion-hearted and to vindicate for the French the right to the title of originators of the "terzine." This and other mistakes of Kauffer were soon corrected.[1] The fragment records part of a legend of St. Madeleine.

2. The text is published by Suchier (who profited by Forster's emendations of the edition of Kauffer) in *Zt. Rom. Phil.* IV, 362–363.

3. The Ms. is of the town library of Trèves.

4. The poet cannot be placed before the beginning of the thirteenth century. The writing of the Ms. seems that of the latter part of the same century.

5. Schmidt, *Roman. Stud.* IV, 540, notes four characteristics of the language: the rhyming of *e : ie*; -EBAT : -ABAT; $\rho : \bar{u}$ (*luis : pluis* from LŎCOS, PLŪS); *ai : e*.

FABLIAU DU HÉRON

1. This piece, of 172 lines, is important because it offers, in all probability, one of the few instances of *fabliaux* of English origin.

2. It is edited by Meyer in *Rom.* XXVI, 88–91: *Le Fabliau du Héron ou de la Fille mal gardée.*

3. This *fabliau* occurs in the same Ms. as the *Aspremont* fragment published by Meyer (cf. p. 29), and follows directly upon it.

4. The copy of the *fabliau* is not, however, by the same hand that wrote the *Aspremont*, but by one apparently a

---

[1] For the whole story, cf. *Rom.* IX, 491.

little later — Meyer suggests the last years of the thirteenth century.

5. The language, too, shows some variations from that of *Aspremont,* and is considered by Meyer (p 88).

LE DONNEI DES AMANTS

1. This is an anonymous poem that cannot be attributed to any of our well-known Anglo-Norman poets, although the author resembles Huon de Rotelande and Chardri in several points. Indeed, the latter seems to have known the *Donnei,* and to have developed an idea from it in his *Petit Plet.* The word "donnei" is derived from Provençal *donnei,* which was formed from *domneiar,* a term meaning to "pay court to the ladies." In our poem, and generally, *donnei* indicates an amorous conversation [1]

2. The poem and a study of it were published by Paris in *Rom.* XXV, 497–541 (the text itself, of 1244 lines, occupies pp. 500–522).

3. The Ms. is from the Phillipps library, Cheltenham, and was written at the end of the thirteenth or beginning of the fourteenth century.[2]

4. Paris thinks the original was written during the last years of the twelfth century.[3]

5. The poem reveals several characteristic Anglo-Norman traits, such as *lenz = laenz; aver: aler; joe =* EGO, etc.[4]

PÈLERINAGE DE CHARLEMAGNE

1. This text is included in my list, as are the *Roland* and the *Alexis,* because of the Anglo-Norman Ms. of it, which, as in the case of the two monuments cited, is easily acces-

---

[1] *Rom.* XXV, 522 and 534. The *Donnei* appears after Chardri in my list because of the difference in the dates of the Mss of the two.

[2] Cf. pp. 497–500.

[3] Cf. p. 534 ; he is sustained in this by Vising, *Jhrsbrcht. Rom. Phil* IV, 1, 297, though Gröber, *Zt.* XXI, 575, prefers the first quarter of the thirteenth. [4] pp. 531–532, and cf Vising, *Jhrsbrcht.* IV, 1, 298.

sible to the student, since it is reproduced in the critical edition of the poem.

2. This edition is that of E. Koschwitz, *Karls des Grossen Reise nach Jerusalem und Constantinopel*, Leipzig, 1900. Fourth ed. (*Altfranz. Bibl.* II).

3. The Anglo-Norman Ms. (of the British Museum), the only one known to contain the *Pèlerinage*, was lost in 1879. Before this date, however, Koch had photographed it, and Wulcker and Nicol had collated Michel's edition (the first) of the poem (1836) founded on this Ms. Koschwitz prints Koch's facsimile in its entirety opposite the critical text, availing himself of variants from the two collations referred to.

4. The Ms., a faulty one, by a scribe but ill acquainted with French, belongs to the end of the thirteenth or the beginning of the fourteenth century.

5. The language of this text was made the subject of an especial study by Koschwitz in his book, *Ueberlieferung und Sprache der Chanson du Voyage de Charlemagne*, Heilbronn, 1876. Here we may find many points of interest for the student of Anglo-Norman.

MISCELLANEOUS POEMS

1, 2. I refer here to the scattered pieces published by Meyer, *Rom.* IV, 370–397, with the title: *Mélanges de Poésie Anglo-Normande*.

3, 4. The names of the pieces, Mss., and dates are the following: —

a (p. 370). *Missus Gabriel;* British Museum Ms. of end of thirteenth century. Here we may include the " *Chanson a boire* " from the same Ms., published by Paris, *Rom.* XXI, 260. It is worth noting that this was the Ms. (now lost) containing the *Pèlerinage* (cf. above).

b (p. 373). *Prière;* Trinity College Ms., of the end of the thirteenth century.

c (p. 374). *Chanson;* Bodleian Library, of the second half of the thirteenth century.

d (p. 385). *États du Monde;* Cambridge Ms., middle of the thirteenth century. This is a most interesting little poem from several points of view. Meyer devotes ten pages to a consideration of it.

e (p. 395). *Plainte;* British Museum, end of thirteenth century.

Of the fourteenth century we have: —

f (p. 375). Three *Chansons* from a Cambridge Ms.

g (p. 383). *Définition de l'Amour* from a Bodleian Ms. In addition, several pieces are printed whose dates are not indicated (pp. 372, 380, and 384).

BIBLE TRANSLATION

1, 2. A fragment of a translation into verse is given by Bonnardot, *Rom.* XVI, 177–213. This fragment consists of 1013 verses.

3, 4. The editor used a Ms. of Trèves, appending variants from two other Mss. of the Bibliothèque Nationale, all three being of the fourteenth century, and all written in England.[1] Meyer, in a note at the end of Bonnardot's article (p. 212), mentions two other Mss. (of Oxford and Cheltenham) containing the translation.

APOCALYPSE

1. This text is important in several ways: similar versions of the Apocalypse were very popular; of the present one in verse there are seven Mss.; of that in prose[2] we know of sixteen; again, it represents a change in taste of the public of the time (end of thirteenth century) in so far as this public no longer cared for imaginative works in themselves, but rather

[1] The language, however, is of a purity that indicates a much earlier date, or else that the copyist had before him an original from the continent.

[2] Published by Meyer and Delisle. *L'Apocalypse en Français au XIIIe Siècle*, Paris, 1901 (*Anc. Tex. Fr.*).

for vulgarizations of what the clerks read in Latin; finally, it is typical of the mediocre poetical works which mark the close of the Anglo-Norman period, — productions incorrect in language and versification; like those of William Waddington, Peter Langtoft, and the author of *Hugo of Lincoln*.[1]

2. The edition here referred to is that of Meyer: *Version Anglo-Normande en Vers de l'Apocalypse*, *Rom.* XXV, 174–257 (texts of 355 and 1431 lines, pp. 187–253).

3. The seven Mss. are described and classified (pp. 175–182) in three families. Meyer publishes the representatives of two of these groups in full, giving selections from the other Mss.[2]

4. The dates of the Mss. vary from the beginning to the middle of the fourteenth century. The date of the original was in the thirteenth century.[3]

5. Meyer, pp. 255–256, speaks of peculiarities of the language.

ST. PAUL

1. The visit of St. Paul to hell, under the conduct of St. Michael, is described in Anglo-Norman versions as it is in practically all other mediæval languages.

2. The version we note is that edited by Meyer in *Rom.* XXIV, 357–375: *La Descente de Saint Paul en Enfer* (text of 282 lines, pp. 365–375).

3. This version is in a single Ms., that of Toulouse, which contained the *Apocalypse* too.

4. The date of the Ms. is about the middle of the fourteenth century, and the composition of the poem was doubtless but little previous to that time.

5. Several peculiarities of the language are mentioned by Meyer (p. 362).

---

[1] *Rom.* XXV, 175, 253, and 257. Vising, in his notice of Meyer's edition (*Jhrsbrcht. Rom Phil* IV, 1, 207), resents the reference to the " close " of the Anglo-Norman period.   [2] Cf. the remarks on p. 184.

[3] Cf. *Rom* XXV, 175 and 186. On p. 186, line 21, is not " XIII⁰ siècle " a misprint for " XIV⁰ siècle "?

BOZON

1. We know little of this writer of both prose and poetry beyond his name, which is spelled in four different ways: Bozon, Boioun, Boson, and Bosoun. Wright indicates [1] that the name was a common one, which fact increases the difficulties of identifying Bozon the writer. Allusions in his *Contes* point to their having been written a little after 1320, and to their author's acquaintance with the North of England.

2. *Les Contes Moralisées de Nicole Bozon, Frère Mineur.* Edited by L. T. Smith and P. Meyer, Paris, 1889 (*Anc. Textes*). A few poems of Bozon are incorporated in this volume and others referred to.

3. The edition is based on a London Ms., with variants from one of Cheltenham. These, together with a Ms. containing a Latin translation of some of the *Contes*, are described, pp. lxvi-lxxiii

4. The date of the Mss. is not later than the middle of the fourteenth century. The date of the original has been alluded to above as after 1320. (The evidence for this date was derived from the *Contes* alone, however; there is no certain indication for the poetry.[2])

5. The language is treated, pp lviii-lxvi.[3]

For convenience of reference in the pages that now follow, I append here a table of the texts arranged in the order just indicated. The term "beginning" includes, approximately, the first forty years of the given century; "middle," from about —40 to about —60; "latter part" from about —60 to the end.

[1] *Biogr. Brit Lit* p. 331   [2] Cf. *Rom.* XXIV, 362, f.-n. 2

[3] On p. lviii, foot-note, the reference is to *Rom.* XII and not XIII. I do not go into details concerning Bozon's language. At his time the irregularities, particularly in orthography, become overwhelming. For the fourteenth century in general we have the dissertation of E. Busch: *Laut und Formenlehre der Anglonormannischen Sprache des XIV Jahrhunderts*, Greifswald, 1887.

TWELFTH CENTURY MIDDLE	Philippe de Thaün *Alexis* *Lois Guillaume*
LATTER PART	*Oxford Psalter* *Cambridge Psalter* *Arundel Psalter* *Quatre Livres des Rois* *Roland* *Brandan* Gaimar
THIRTEENTH CENTURY BEGINNING	Adgar Fantosme Angier Chardri Guillaume de Berneville *Modwenne*
MIDDLE	*Vie St. Thomas* *Adam* *Boeve* *Amadas* *Chevalier, Dame et Clerc* *Auban* *Sardenai* *Aspremont*
LATTER PART	*Madeleine* *Fabliau du Héron* *Donnei des Amants* *Pèlerinage Charlemagne* *Mélanges de Poésie*
FOURTEENTH CENTURY BEGINNING AND MIDDLE	*Bible Fragment* *Apocalypse* *Descente St. Paul* Bozon

III. PHONOLOGY AND MORPHOLOGY

I now approach that portion of my task which will inevitably lend itself to criticism, correction, and completion. First of all, I have tried to do what has not been done before, — to construct a grammar of Anglo-Norman, not as a means of comparison of known developments with those of some text to be edited, but a grammar of the dialect as a whole. I divide this part into appropriate headings and sections just as if it were the grammar of a most important language.   Whatever may be the disadvantages of this scheme, it pretends to one advantage: the student can discover quickly what the Anglo-Norman treatment of various phenomena was, whether important or not.   It goes without saying that, at my distance from sources, I have not been able to base my statements on personal examination of the Mss. involved.   I have often depended on studies of the language of the different texts by writers who are not always authorities, perhaps, and who, in any case, are not always careful to distinguish between language of author and of scribe.   Some of these studies (already referred to in my bibliography of texts), especially those on the earlier texts, are doctors' dissertations, which are to be quoted with caution because, as first attempts, they often betray the inexperience — in no way blameworthy — of their authors, these monographs I have endeavored to control by consulting the published texts for myself, and by a careful collation of the given dissertations with the important reviews of them (to which reviews I have likewise made reference in my bibliography).

PHONOLOGY

A

1. FREE A > E.

1. Quality of the E < A. Here we enter upon one of the fundamental questions of Old French philology. Early in the history of our subject it was seen that we have to deal with three different *e's*: $e <$ A, $e < \breve{e}$, and $e < \bar{e}$ or $\breve{i}$. The distinction among them is undeniable, but as to the exact value of each of the three no definite result has been attained. In brief, $e <$ A assonances only with itself (or with an $e < \breve{e}$ which has not diphthongized in free position, as *deus, eret*), so that this $e <$ A is neither open nor close in the sense that $e < \bar{e}$ or $\breve{e}$ was close or open.[1]

In Anglo-Norman this $e <$ A (and here we have to include the *e* of the reduced diphthong *ie*, cf. p. 55) is to be considered close, for the earlier monuments at least. The bibliography on this point is quite one-sided.[2] The ultimate confusion in Anglo-Norman rhyme of close $e <$ A with an open *e* reflects the similar condition of affairs on the

---

[1] A general idea of the points of the question may be had from consulting the following references : Paris, *Rom.* IV, 499, VII, 122 ; Such. *Zt.* III, 137 ; Meyer-Lubke, *Gram.* I, 213, § 225 ; Nyrop, *Gram.* I, 153 ; Such. *Gram.* p. 24.

[2] We note the first definite statements for Anglo-Norman by Suchier, *Zt* II, 293, III, 140. Cf. *Zt.* III, 593 (Mussafia) ; Uhlemann, in his work on *Auban, Roman. Stud.* IV, 563, questions the close *e* ; he suggests that its value may have varied at different periods of Anglo-Norman, or according to accented or unaccented position. Suchier, *Litblt.* III, 15, disproves this, and adheres to his idea that *e* was close in every position up to the end of the twelfth century. Cf. Vising, *Étude*, p. 68.

Continent The tendency to confusion was especially, and maybe first, manifested in the case of $e + l$ or r.[1]

2. ORTHOGRAPHIC VARIANTS OF E < A. The two most important and frequently recurring variants are *ie* and *ei*, both found in a number of the earliest texts and appearing, with greater or less frequency, throughout the entire Anglo-Norman period. They are to be noted, too, because it has been claimed that they represented, in some cases at least, real phonetic values

a. *ie*. A few examples for this are the following: *Cumpoz*, *cliers* (CLARUS) 3006, *piert* (PARET) 2509 (both Ms. L); *Camb. Psalt. remembriere* (LXXIII, 18, 22), *abitiere* (XXI, 3) and the like.[2] Instances in the *Camb. Psalt.* seem confined to derivates of -ATOR. Chardri, *Petit Plet*, *tiel*, 216, 451; *Boeve*, *tiel*, 3564, 3830 (Ms. D). Full lists of examples are given by Sturzinger[3] and Stimming.[4]

The first explanation we note here is that of Mall[5] to the effect that since Continental *ie* early lost its value as a diphthong in Anglo-Norman (cf. below, p. 55), the scribes did not have a definite knowledge as to the proper use of the *ie*; in their efforts to write a correct French, they replaced their Anglo-Norman *e* by *ie*, but gave no thought to the etymological background of their *e*; consequently we find in Anglo-Norman this *ie* representing not only the regular development of Popular Latin open E, but also substituted for $e <$ A and $e <$ Ē. Schumann (p. 14), with an eye to the class of words (<-ATOR) peculiar to his text (*Camb. Psalt.*), thought that words of the type of *remembriere* were analo-

---

[1] Cf. p 48, "$a + l$ or r" for references and examples. Cf. also Meyer-Lubke, *Gram* I, 214, § 226

[2] Schumann, p. 14. (For the full titles of works referred to, as here, by a mere name, I expect the student to refer to my text bibliography above. In this way he will become familiar with the monuments and works and workers on them For example, here he will look under *Camb. Psalt.* p. 14, § 5, studies on the language.)

[3] *Orth. Gall.* pp. 39–40.   [4] *Boeve*, p. 176.

[5] *Cumpoz*, p. 69.

gous to others like *jugierre*, in which *ie* was a regular
phonetic development. The explanation of Mall seems
more in accord with what we should expect of the average
Anglo-Norman scribe.[1]

The suggestion that the *ie* might represent a phonetic
change was Suchier's;[2] he based it on English *friar* < *frère*
(FRATREM). Stimming, however,[3] claims that *friar*, *briar*,
and the like originated in South England, where close *e*
regularly becomes *i* and *ei*, and that the *a* was a glide sound
between these and the *r*.

On the relative ages of *ie* and *ee*, see below, p. 41.

b. *ei*. Examples for *ei* are very numerous, beginning
with the earliest texts; for instance, *Oxf. Psalt.*[4] *seit* (SAPIT)
LXXII, 11, LXXXVIII, 15, *seis*, LXVIII, 4; *Camb. Psalt.*[5]
espeie, XLIII, 3, 6, *incurveie*, XXXIV, 15; Gaimar, *leveiz*,
1383; *Dialog. Greg. aleir*, *remaneir*, *acheveir*, and the like.[6]

Verb forms, like those just cited from Angier and Gaimar,
swelled the number of examples of this phenomenon; since
-*eir* verbs so frequently become -*er* in Anglo-Norman (cf.
p. 119), scribes were confused as to the correct usage of -*eir*
and -*er*. In examples not drawn from verb forms we have
to do with an uncertainty of the scribes, like that in the case
of *ie*; that is, since *ei* (< close Popular Latin E) was reduced to *e* in Anglo-Norman (cf. p. 52), the scribes, in their
efforts to restore *ei*, substituted it for every *e*, whatever the
origin of *e*.

Suchier[7] considered this *ei* as a graphic variant, but here
again Stimming[8] disagrees with him, saying there is evidence that *ei* was a diphthong.[9]

---

[1] Cf. Meyer-Lubke, *Gram.* I, 173, § 179; Sturzinger, *Orth. Gall.* pp.
38–39, 41 (here we find a bibliography for the history of the *ie*).

[2] *Gram.* p. 23.   [3] *Boeve*, pp. 176, 181.

[4] Harseim, p. 277.   [5] Schumann, p. 15.

[6] Cloran, p. 40.   [7] *Gram.* p. 24.   [8] *Boeve*, p. 175.

[9] Rhymes from *Dialog. Greg.* may indicate the same. Cf. Cloran,
p. 40.

c. *oi*. This orthography may be counted as a variant of the *ei* just treated; it is used for words in which *ei* replaced *e* < A, and is an extension of the *oi* for *ei* < ᶒ (cf. p 50). The only examples noted are for the *Dialog. Greg.*[1]

d. *ee*. A few examples here are *Cumpoz, peert* (Ms C, 2519); *Bestiaire, seet, eet, plentee* (Walberg, LXXXIV); Gaimar, *leez*, 665; Chardri, *Pet. Plet, seet* (Ms. V, 172).[2]

Here again the first explanation we note is that of Mall,[3] who speaks of the use of *ee* or *éé* as a variation of *ie*; that is, the scribe desired to indicate a sound other than that of *e*, but did not want to use *ie*. This remark is quoted by Suchier[4] in refutation of Uhlemann, who, in upholding his claim for an open pronunciation of *e* < A, cited the orthography *ee* (of the *Auban*) as indicating an open *e*. Mall thought of it as pointing to close, lengthened *e*. Sturzinger[5] makes some interesting remarks upon the relative ages of *ee* and *ie*, though what he says may appear somewhat contradictory. In his discussion of *ee* < free open ᴇ, he says that *ee* was not a stage preceding *ie*, but was so used to denote the length of the vowel (*i e.* of *e* which Anglo-Norman used for *ie*), after the fashion of English orthography of the fourteenth century. Then he says that *ee* = *e* = A fell in phonetically with *ee* = *ie* = ᶒ, and by false analogy to the latter, the former *ee* was likewise written *ie*. Thus here (in the case of *ee* = *e* = A) *ee* must have preceded *ie*; in the other case (*ee* = ᶒ), *ee* must have followed *ie* If, however, *ee* was fashioned after English orthography of the fourteenth century to indicate the length of *e* in one instance, it seems reasonable to suppose that it was used at this time to denote the length of all *e*'s, regardless of their provenance. If, again, *ee* was thus late in its diffusion, it probably had little to do with the origin of *ie* = *e* = A, a better explanation of

---

[1] Cloran, p. 40.

[2] Texts and examples, Stimming, *Boeve*, p 175; Sturzinger, *Orth Gall* pp 40-41. [3] *Cumpoz*, p 69

[4] *Litblt.* III, 16 (cf. *Zt.* III, 477). [5] *Orth Gall.* p 40.

which has already been suggested (p. 39). Difficulty will be experienced in establishing comparative dates for such phenomena, since we have to base our arguments on the usage of scribes who so easily confused spellings. The simplest statement to be made is doubtless this: *ee* was used to indicate close *e*; this close *e* was that < A and that < *ie* < ẹ; the *ee* was independent of *ie* < ẹ (and, of course, of *ie* as used for *e* < A); there is no evidence pointing to any progression in the phonetic development of the sounds denoted by *ee* and *ie*, or in the use of these signs by the scribes.

e. *ae* or *oe*. Examples for *ae* have been noted in *Auban:* saet (SAPIT),[1] *Vie Greg.:* aeve (ACQUA);[2] *Camb. Psalt. paerre*, XXXVIII, 14.

Uhlemann[1] adduced *ae* as a further proof of the open value he wished to assign to the *e* < A. Suchier[3] again refuses to accept this idea, saying that *ae* is only an orthographical ornament used as an alternative for *e*, just as *y* is used for *i* (cf. p. 65) — both without any especial phonetic value. He reverts to this again in his *Grammatik*,[4] referring there to *oe* (as well as *ae*) as an alternative for *e*. Meyer,[2] however, seems to understand *ae* as indicating the open sound of *e* in his text. (See further *ae* = *ai* under *a* + palatal, p. 45, and *ae* = *e* < *ei* < ẹ, p. 52.)

f. *a*. Examples for this are noted by Suchier;[5] as, *Camb. Psalt.* avortad; *Quatre Liv. R.:* strae (for *estree*); he says such words are either scribal errors, or else to be explained each by itself. Stimming[6] notes *estat* in *Boeve*.

g. *i*. With the exception of *til* = *tel*, Denis Pyramus, *Vie St. Edmond*, 654,[7] examples seem to be confined to the pret-

---

[1] Uhlemann, p. 562.   [2] *Rom.* XII, 194.
[3] *Litblt.* III, 16.   [4] p. 19.
[5] *Gram.* p 23.   [6] *Boeve*, p. 176.
[7] My examples from this text are drawn from the edition of Arnold in *Memorials of St. Edmond's Abbey*, London, 1892. Vol. II, pp. 137 *ss.* [A new edition of the *Vie* is now being prepared.]

erite and past participle *remis* or *mist* (RIMASUS, MASIT), obviously analogical. Stimming gives texts and references.[1]

h. ai. *ai* really does not belong here, as it is not a variant of *e* in orthography, but of an *a* which has remained, for whatever reason. It has nothing in common with the *a* noted above (under f). It seems to be a peculiarity of fourteenth-century texts, though in atonic position it occurs at a much earlier date (cf p 50) Stimming[2] gives examples like *lerrai* for *lerra, ai* for *a* (HABET).

i. eo. *eo* for close *e* corresponds to *ea* for open *e*. It is comparatively late; cf. below, p. 57, § 13.

2. A BEFORE A PALATAL.

The history of the developments here is interesting because some of them are limited to Anglo-Norman territory and because several of the most important are to be observed in Anglo-Norman before they make their appearance in continental French. We find in our texts that *ai* has the value of *ẹi*, or else that of *ẹ* in pronunciation and that *ei* and *e* occur with great frequency in orthography, though not to the exclusion of *ai* which is found particularly in the older prose texts, as the *Psalters* and *Lois Guillaume*, and doubtless there represents the original pronunciation (*ái*). Anglo-Norman poets, however, without regard to the value of *ai* as *ái, ei,* or *e* (cf. below), used it, at times, in rhyme with *i* (*pais : dis,* Denis Pyramus).

1. EI AND E. We note the former in *Bestiaire*,[3] *Lois Guillaume, Oxf. Psalt , Quatre Liv. R., Brandan,* Gaimar, Angier, and *Boeve;* the latter in *Cumpoz, Bestiaire*,[3] *Domesday Book*,[4] *Lois Guillaume, Camb. Psalt., Q. L. R., Brandan,* Gaimar, Angier, Chardri, Gme. de Berneville, *Boeve, Sardenai* (*leisse : confesse,* 241), *Donnei* (p. 532). Some of the discussion here is worthy of attention. Mall[5]

---

[1] *Boeve,* p. 176 ; cf. below, § 66, 2.
[2] *Ibid.* p. 172.   [3] Walberg, pp. xlviii, lxxxv, xliv.
[4] *Zt.* VIII, 358.   [5] *Cumpoz,* p. 59.

mentions three cases from his text and four from the *Bestiaire* in which *a* + a palatal is represented by *e*, all the examples showing *ai* + *str*;[1] he says the *e* shows that the character of the *ai* as a diphthong was being modified at the time of these texts and was approaching the value of *ę*. Six years after Mull's statement had been made, Grober[2] seems to wish to combat a tendency then prevalent to place the general reduction of *ai* at too early a date. He says the monophthongization took place in the works of Philippe de Thaun on account of the phonetically difficult (and long) consonant group following the *ai* (*maistre, paistre*) and not from a general tendency in that direction. The nature and date of the development attracted much attention about the time of Grober's note,[3] and after this time we observe that editors and grammarians study the *ai* with reference to its position before consonant, or vowel, or consonant group, or final, and the like. For example, Paris establishes the following for Gme. de Berneville:[4] *ai* is distinct from *ei*, both final and before a consonant. *Ait*:[5] *eit* only once (3307) nor does *ain* : *ein*; but *mais* : *pres, lairme* : *terme, faire* : *terre*. The value of the latter *ai* is *ę*. If we draw up a table formulated from Paris's remarks, we shall have the following:—

e < ton. check. *ę*: *ai* + Cons.

e < ton. check. *ę* does not rhyme with *e* < Ē, ĭ.

e < ton. check. *ę* and *e* < Ē, ĭ do not rhyme with *e* < A.

(Incidentally we note the three *e*'s in his text.)

In Vising, *Étude*, pp. 75, 84, and 93, we note the following: in *Brandan*, Gaimar and Fantosme, *ai* : *ei* before nasals. Under other circumstances there are variations: *Brandan ; ai* not : *ei*.

---

[1] Cf. Walberg, p. xliv.   [2] *Zt.* III, 451, f.-n.

[3] References to several important articles are given by Neumann, *Litblt.* IV, 18. Add to these his own clear statement, *Zt.* XIV, 569.

[4] p. xxvii.

[5] I use this sign [:] to indicate "rhyming with," "rhymes with," etc.

ai : *e* (once, *termes* : *lermes*, 891). Gaimar; *ei* not : *ai*;[1] *ei*
not : *e*; *ai* : *e*. Fantosme; *ai* : *e* often;[2] *ei* : *e* seldom; *ei* : *ai*;[3]
ei : *e*.

From this state of affairs Vising concludes that *ai* became
a monophthong (*e*) before *ei* did. [This to explain *ai* not :
ei, and *ei* not : *e*] When we do find *ai* . *ei*, it is after both
had become monophthongs. If Vising means that *ai* and *ei*
went different ways in developing into *e*, he may not be
right; it seems more likely that *ai* passed through the *ei*
stage before simplification to *e*.[4] Suchier mentions as characteristic of Anglo-Norman the contraction in a free syllable; likewise the endings *ai*, *aie*, continue as diphthongs in
this dialect. We note an example of the latter usage in
Boeve,[5] where *ai* rhymes with *ei* (< ε); as *sai* : *mei*, etc.

2. ORTHOGRAPHIC VARIANTS OF AI, EI, E.

a. *ee*. This variant is spoken of at length by Sturzinger,[6]
who says it is phonetically different from the *ee* < ε and the
ee < *e* (< A), and that it is never written *ie*. He gives examples from Gaimar, Chardri, Langtoft, and others. Stimming[7] adds a few: *pees* (PACEM), *fees* (FASCEM), and the like.

b. *a*. This occurs with some frequency; many of the
examples are those of verb terminations where -*ai* has been
replaced by -*a*[8] (*fra* = *ferai*, *sa* = *sai*, etc.), also *fare*, *fates*,
plase, and the like. Stimming[7] refers to texts. Cloran[9] adds
three examples from his text.

c. *ae*. This has been noted only for Angier,[10] and examples seem confined to closed syllables (*paestre*, *maestre*, etc.).

d. *oi*. This occurs often in Angier[9] (*foit*, *soie*, *porroi*,

---

[1] Cf. here Kupferschmidt, p. 417.

[2] Chardri's usage is similar to that of Fantosme, cf. Vising, *Étude*,
p. 75, Such. *Lublt.* III, 17.

[3] In *aine*, *eine*, *aire*, *eire*, and not when final, Such. *Auban*, p
4, *Lublt.* III, 17.

[4] For detailed statement cf. Such. *Gram.* pp 37–39

[5] Stimming, p. viii   [6] *Orth. Gall.* p 41.   [7] *Boeve*, p. 195.

[8] For the opposite process (*a* > *ai*), cf. p. 43

[9] *Dialog. Greg* p. 42.   [10] Meyer, p. 193, Cloran, p. 41.

etc.), and is not limited to words in which the *ai* follows a labial.[1] An instance occurs in *Mélanges*[2] (cf. p. 32), *soi* = SAPIO.

e. *aei*. This seems very rare. There is an example in the *Arundel Psalt. paeis*,[3] and Cloran[4] notes two (*traeit, vaeis*) in the *Dialog. Greg.* Here the *aei* = *ei* (which in Angier is more frequent than *ai*), the *ae* being equivalent to the *e* (cf. p. 42).

f. *ea*. Here I have noted only *eat* = *ait* < HABET in *Articuli Willelmi*[5] (cf. p. 57, *ea* for checked ẹ).

3. A BEFORE L MOUILLÉE.

Anglo-Norman belongs to the dialects which change *al'e* > *el'e*. This occurs in *Q. L. R.* before the accent only; later in accented syllables.[6]

4. A BEFORE A NASAL.

1. FREE POSITION.

a. *ain* and *ein*. These two do not rhyme in *Cumpoz* and *Bestiaire*, nor in the *Vie St. Gilles*.[7] In the other poetical texts they do.[8] In prose texts *ei* and *ai* interchange from the beginning. In *Oxf. Psalt.*, for example, *ai* occurs even for etymological *ei* (*fain, rain*). In *Lois Guillaume ei* occurs but three times (two of these in atonic syllable).[9] In Anglo-Norman the early confusion of *ain* and *ein* is characteristic; the ẽi became ãi in pronunciation in the middle of the twelfth century, and after that time the two were used promiscuously in orthography.[10]

---

[1] Cf. Such. *Gram.* p. 39, e.   [2] *Rom.* IV, 377.
[3] *Zt.* XII, 24.   [4] *Dialog. Greg.* p. 42.   [5] *Zt.* XIX, 81, f.-n. 10.
[6] Meyer-Lübke, *Gram.* I, 219, § 232.
[7] Mall, p. 59; Walberg, p. xlviii; Paris, p. xxvii; Vising, *Litblt.* IV, 311.
[8] References in Stimming, *Boeve*, p. 196.   [9] Matzke, p. xliii.
[10] Such. *Gram.* p. 72; (in) Gröber's *Grundriss*, I, 572; *Français et Provençal*, p. 23.

b. *ain* and *aine*. It is worth noting that these two rhyme in late Anglo-Norman (as *fontaine* : *lendemain*).[1]

c. *en*. Examples of *en* for *ain* are rare in earlier Anglo-Norman. In *Q. L. R.* we see *enz*; in *Roland, marrenes*. A few others, including some from *Boeve*, are given by Stimming[2] In the *Apocalypse, ain, ein,* and *en* have but one sound, and in Bozon *en* is even written for *ai* (*grendre*) and *ei* (*mendre*).[3]

d *an*. This seems more frequent for *ain* than does *en*, and occurs in rhyme several times, as *ahan . pan* (PANEM), *Adam;* also in proper names, as *Johan* : *Abraam*.[4]

2 CHECKED POSITION. The most interesting phenomenon we encounter here is the appearance of *au* for *a +* nasal + consonant . *quaunt, davaunt, graunt,* and the like. The first examples accurately dated are given by Sturzinger,[5] the earliest being of 1266. Still earlier, however, may be those given by Koch[6] from Ms. L of Chardri (first half of the thirteenth century) We may say, in a general way, that the *a +* nasal + consonant became *au* during the second part of the thirteenth century. Note, for example, the remark of Meyer[7] in connection with the *Fabliau du Héron*, to the effect that it is not surprising to find in the latter part of a manuscript (written at the end of the thirteenth century), *aun* and *oun* which do not occur in the poems of the earlier

---

[1] Examples and references, Meyer, *Rom.* XXV, 255.

[2] p 197 ; cf. Such. *Gram* p 71.

[3] *Rom* XXV, 256 , *Bozon*, p. lix.

[4] Such. *Gram* p. 71, Stimming, *Boeve*, p. 197 ; Walberg, p xli ; Cloran, p. 43   [5] *Orth. Gall.* p xxxix.

[6] pp. vi and xxx. Meyer-Lubke, *Gram.* I, 227, § 245, speaks of examples from Ms O, which is later than L Koch specifically cites *aun* of Ms. L, while avowing that it is rare. Cf. also Such *Gram.* p. 67 ; Stimming, *Boeve*, p. 173 , and Uhlemann, *Auban*, p. 559. Stimming probably errs in including Angier's works among texts showing *aun*, since Meyer, p. 193, says *aun* does not occur in *Vie Greg.*, nor does Cloran (p. 43) cite an instance for the *Dialogues*.

[7] *Rom.* XXVI, 88.

part of the same Ms. (written in the middle of the thirteenth century).

The origin and nature of this *aun* have not been definitely established. Koschwitz first suggested[1] that the diphthong arose after $a + l$ + consonant had become *au*,— it was equivalent to a + a *u*-glide ("nachklang"). We note no further discussion till twenty years later, when Sheldon touches upon the point,[2] proposing a phonetical explanation based on the result of the contact on English territory of the French and English pronunciations of a and of nasal consonants. Many questions are to be raised in a study of this problem, and the whole demands extended treatment.[3]

ain. I have noted one example of *ai* in checked position, — that in *Arundel Psalt., caímp.*[4]

5. A BEFORE L OR R.

For the endings -ALEM, -ALUM we note hesitation in Anglo-Norman between a and e. Examples are given by Suchier[5] and Walberg:[6] *tal, mal, mortal*, etc. We find *tal* in *Vie Greg.*[7] and *al* in general in *Adam.*[8] This tendency for -*al* is Norman and Anglo-Norman.[9] In cases where *al* does become *el*, poets may treat this *el* as *ęl*[10] (this forming the exception to the general $ę <$ A in Anglo-Norman, cf. p. 38). The same confusion exists for $ę$ and $ę$ before *r*. Notable examples are to be seen in the *Donnei des Amants:*[11] *manere : contrefere; chanter : quer;* identical rhymes are not cited outside of Anglo-Norman. Even the $e < ai + r$ may be

[1] *Ueberlieferung* (full reference above, p. 32), p. 21.

[2] *Child Memorial Volume*, Boston, 1896, pp. 69–76.

[3] Cf. the remarks on Sheldon's paper by Paris, *Rom.* XXVII, 320, and by Vising, *Jhrsbrcht. Rom. Phil.* V, 2, p. 289.

[4] *Zt.* XI, 520 ; in the same text occurs *cam ; Zt.* XII, 50.

[5] *Gram.* p. 22.   [6] *Bestiaire*, p. xli.

[7] Lines 2699, 2767, for example.

[8] Grass, p. 111.   [9] *Rom.* XXI, 261.

[10] Such. *Gram.* p. 25 ; Stimming, *Boeve*, pp. liv, lvii.

[11] *Rom.* XXV, 532.

treated as close.[1] Obviously, Anglo-Norman did not demand
an open vowel before *r*; phonetic principles seem to play no
part here. Cases of rhymes (or assonances) in -*er* came up
frequently, particularly because of numbers of infinitive
forms (in original -*er* and in -*er* < -*eir*). This -*er* was treated
by the poet as -*ẹr* or -*ẹr* according to the needs of his
verse.

6. A PRETONIC.

1. Loss of A in Hiatus. The most noteworthy point
in connection with pretonic *a* is the possibility of its loss in
hiatus; examples are very few, but in any case they have
not been found in texts other than Anglo-Norman, according
to Paris,[2] who cites *lenz* = *laenz* for the *Donnei*, 695, Adgar
and Chardri. We note that in the latter's *Josaphaz*, line
2621, Ms. L has *lens* by the side of Ms. O *leyns*.[3] In *Vie
Greg.*, line 437, an *i* is inserted to break the hiatus, *laienz*.
Is not *cheles* (< *chaeles*, QUID VELLES[4]) *Brandan*, 343, another
instance of the contraction? Cf. a similar contraction of
pretonic *e* (*leale* > *lele*) on p. 60.

2. A replaced by Other Letters. a. *e* for *a*. The
use of *e* in cases like *essalt, rechata*, seems much favored in
Anglo-Norman;[5] we note, too, that before *r* + consonant,
pretonic *a* > *e* with great frequency : *mercher, herneis*, etc.[6]
It seems, nevertheless, that cases in which *a* remains are the
more frequent, and instances of phonetic *e* > *a* are not lacking ; cf., for example, *chaval* of the *Cambridge* and *Arundel
Psalters*, and in the latter text *e* + *s* + consonant often
becomes *a*; as, *asperunt, aster, astrainge* [7] (cf. p. 62, pretonic *e*).

---

[1] Stimming, p. 193.   [2] *Rom* XXV, 531.

[3] Koch, *Variants*, p 186.   [4] Such., *Zt.* I, 428.

[5] Citations, Stimming, p. 172. We may add to his list Such. *Auban*,
p. 37 ; Schlosser, *Q. L. R* p. 7.

[6] Pretonic *e* + *r* + consonant > -*ar* is not constant in general French
either. Cf. Nyrop, *Gram.* I, 206.   [7] *Zt.* XII, 28, 35.

E

b. *ai* for *a, vaillet, maitinet,* etc. For citations here, cf. Stimming, *Boeve,* p. 172.

c. *o, au* for *a, ovesques, chaustel,* etc. Cf. Stimming, p. 173.

3. PRETONIC A+PALATAL. Here the favorite orthography seems to be *ei; reisun, teisez,* etc.[1] I have noted one example of *ae* as variant of the *e* of *ei* (cf. pp. 42 and 46) in *Sardenai* (L), line 98. *traeisist.* Besides *ei* we find *a* (*esmaez, aez,* etc), and of course the regular *ai* and *e.*

4. PRETONIC A + NASAL. As variants of *a* here we find *ain* (*ein*), *e* and *o.*[2] The *aun* of accented nasal *a* is to be seen quite as often in the pretonic syllable (*demaunder, saunte,* etc.).[3]

Ẹ

7. FREE Ẹ.

A proper classification of the developments here would be that of *ei, ai, e,* on the one hand, and *oi* on the other, because *ei, ai, e,* represent the real Anglo-Norman products of free Ẹ, while *oi* was an imitation of continental usage. Then, too, *ei, ai, e,* denote a phonetic series : *ei* became *ai* (especially in the endings *-eis, -eise, -eire, -eide, -eit, -eite*) before *ai* (< *a* +palatal) had become *ę*; then *ai* (< *ęi*) fell in with *ai* (< *a*+ palatal) and became *ę,* too.[4] From the time of the earliest texts, however, *oi* occurs sporadically, and a given writer may use *ei, ai,* and *oi,* assigning to all the same value, or else he may make distinctions among them. On account of this inconsistent usage, it is convenient to classify the phenomena differently from what we indicated above. We shall, therefore, treat first of *ei, ai, oi;* then of *e.*

1. EI, AI, OI. In Philippe de Thaun no *ei : oi,* nor, for

---

[1] Examples and texts, Stimming, *Boeve,* pp. 194, 196 ; Meyer-Lubke, *Gram.* I, 302, § 356.

[2] Stimming, pp. 174, 196. Add *Arundel Psalt. maingerent, Zt.* XII, 7, *Otinel, commonde,* 48.

[3] Stimming, *l.c.* Add to texts *Amadas et Ydoine* (*Zt.* XIII, 86).

[4] Cf. Stimming, *Boeve,* pp. 197–199, Such. *Gram.* p. 49.

that matter, does *ei* : *e*.[1] For Angier we have the following
conclusions: in the *Vie*, Meyer[2] is not sure that *ei* and *oi*
represent the same sound; they do not appear to be used
entirely by chance, a preference being shown for *oi*, for example, when the diphthong was immediately followed by
an *e*. In other cases there is hesitation (*mei* and *moi*, en-
gleis and *englois*), but Meyer thinks that the pronunciation of
Angier was doubtless better indicated by *ei*. Cloran, noting
the same confusion of *ei* and *oi* in the *Dialogues*, attempts a
detailed study to show in what parts of verb or pronoun the
one or the other predominates; *ai* occurs too, especially in
rhyme words (*trais*, *vaire*, etc.), rarely in the imperfect tense.[3]

In Chardri [*Chevalier, Dame et Clerc*, and *Adam*] rhymes
like *voie* : *joie* indicate the value of the combination.[4]

In Gine de Berneville the *ei* remains intact and is not confused with *ai* nor *oi* whether final or followed by a consonant.[5] In *Boeve* there is complete assimilation of *ai* and *ei*,
oi too being known to the author.[6] In *Auban ei*, *ai*, and *oi*
occur, though the second is infrequent. In this connection
Uhlemann notes[7] that in Anglo-Norman *ei* for etymological
ai is frequent, the reverse rare, he suggests as a reason for
this that *ei* appealed to the eye as indicating the sound it
represented, and it does not give place to *ai*; on the other
hand we do find *ei* for *ai* because *ei* looks as if it represented
better (than *ai*) the sound of *ai* (which was *ẹi* or *ẹ*). It is
to be questioned whether this was the mental process of the
Anglo-Norman scribes. A contemporary of the writer of
the *Auban* (the scribe of *Amadas*) uses *ai* for *ei* consistently,[8]
and rhymes *ai* and *oi* (*sousferrai* : *otroi*, etc). Toward the
end of the Anglo-Norman period *oi* and *ai* are used indiscriminately,[9] as in Bozon.[10]

---

[1] Walberg, p xlviii.　　[2] Edition, p. 196.　　[3] Cloran, pp. 44 and 46.
[4] Koch, p. xxviii; Meyer, p. 243, Grass, p. 126.
[5] Paris, p xxx　　　　　[6] Stimming, p viii.　　　[7] p. 581.
[8] Andresen, p. 86.
[9] As on the Continent, cf *Zt* III, 389　　　　　　[10] p. lix.

2. E. *e* by the side of *ei* appears in most of our earliest texts; first of all in some of the proper names of the *Domesday Book*.[1] The *e* is apparently unknown to Philippe, though examples occur in some of the Mss.[2] In the *Lois Guillaume e* is the exception even in infinitives.[3] It is found in *Oxf. Psalt.* and *Q. L. R.* especially in infinitives and imperfects (*aver, complaisee*),[4] in *Oxf. Roland* and Gaimar,[5] Angier[6] (*ere*, ITER; *set*, SIAT; *redde*, RIGIDUS); Chardri,[7] *Boeve*[8] (where the *e* rhymes with both *e* and *ę*), *Amadas*,[9] *Donnei*,[10] etc.

3. ORTHOGRAPHIC VARIANTS OF E, EI, OI.

a. Of *e* (*ee, ie, i, oe*). As *e* occurs so frequently for *ei* we may look for the same variants here as those for *e* < A, since we need not expect the Anglo-Norman scribe to think of the origin of his *e*'s. The two most important variants of *e* < A do occur here; that is, *ee* and *ie*,[11] the former being by far the more frequent. One example of *ie, fiez* (= *feiz, fois*), may be considered as analogous to *fiede; fieble* and *endieble* of the *Camb. Psalt.* and *Q. L. R.* are general Old French forms, though found especially in Norman and Anglo-Norman texts.[12] *i* is frequent for *e* in pretonic position (cf. p. 62), and a few examples of the same in tonic position are found,[13] *vodrient, fiz* (*fois*).

oe (*ae*) occurs for any *e* in Anglo-Norman (cf. p. 42) and we find it for *e* < *ei*; many examples are to be noted in the *Q. L. R.* (*moeis, quoe, loe,* etc.).[14]

b. Of *ei, oi* (*eai, aei, ui*). Here the examples are very few : *eai* has been noted only for *Boeve*[15] (*oreayl, creai,* etc.);

---

[1] *Zt* VIII, 358.   [2] Mall, p. 60 ; Walberg, p. xlviii.

[3] Matzke, p. xlvi.

[4] Harseim, p. 283 ; *Zt.* I, 569, II, 482 ; Schlösser, pp. 3, 32, 33.

[5] Stimming, p. 198.   [6] Meyer, p. 195 ; Cloran, p. 45.

[7] Koch, p. xxviii.   [8] Stimming, p viii.

[9] Andresen, p. 85.   [10] Paris, p. 532.

[11] Texts, Stimming, *Boeve*, pp. 198 and 199.

[12] Such. *Gram.* p. 49 , Meyer-Lubke, *Gram.* I, 125, § 115.

[13] Stimming, p. 200.   Cf. below, p. 54 (*e* + nasal).

[14] Cf. Plahn, p. 5.   [15] Stimming, p. 199.

in the *Pèlerinage*, line 253, I note *saei* (*soi*); for *ui* I have found only *sui* (= *soi* sᴇ), *Arundel Psalt.*[1]

8. CHECKED Ẹ.

We find that the distinction between checked ẹ and ę before oral consonants was observed by Philippe,[2] but already in the *Brandan* the confusion appears.[3]

1. Oᴋᴛʜᴏɢʀᴀᴘʜɪᴄ Vᴀʀɪᴀɴᴛs (*ee, ei, eo*). I have noted examples for *ee* in one of the earliest and one of the latest texts: *Arundel Psalt. neez* (ɴɪᴛɪᴅᴜᴍ),[4] *Apocalypse, seeth* (sᴇᴘᴛᴇᴍ), 11, 15, 58, etc. The presence of the *ee* for a shortened ẹ is remarkable in that *ee* is usually considered as a means of denoting lengthening (cf. the remarks on the *ee* < *e* < ᴀ on p. 41). We find *ei*, too, in early and in late texts: *Brandan, oiseil, rocheit*, etc , *Gaimar, valeiz*, etc. ;[5] *eo* is noted in the *Camb. Psalt. feorm, enfeorm*[6] (cf. p. 54 *eo* < ę + *l* or *r*).

9. E BEFORE L MOUILLÉE.

Suchier,[7] after noting the oft-cited *conseil* which occurs in an *ei* assonance of the *Roland*, says that in late Anglo-Norman *el'* was pronounced as *ei-l, ai-l* (*counsail*, Eng. *counsel*) Walberg[8] seems to have made an especial study of this point and claims that *ei* of *eil* was used as a diphthong in early Anglo-Norman too; as, for example, in the *Bestiaire, Brandan*, and Gaimar.

10. Ẹ BEFORE A NASAL.

1. Fʀᴇᴇ Pᴏsɪᴛɪᴏɴ.

a. *ain, ein, en*. Here we may refer to the notes on free *a* + nasal (p. 46) for the confusion of *ain* and *ein*;[9] *e* occurs, too (cf. p. 47), and as early as Gaimar we note *meins: tens*,[10] 1811.

[1] *Zt.* XI, 517.   [2] Walberg, p. xliii.
[3] Such. *Gram.* p. 21 ; Meyer-Lübke, *Gram.* I, 121, § 111.
[4] *Zt.* XII, 30.   [5] Stimming, *Boeve*, p. 175.   [6] *Orth. Gal.* p 45.
[7] *Gram.* p. 21.   [8] *Bestiaire*, pp. xlix, l.
[9] Texts, Stimming, *Boeve*, p. 201.   [10] Kupferschmidt, p. 417.

b. Variants (*oei, eie, i*). In *Q. L. R.* we note *moeine*[1] (cf. p. 42); in *eie* the last *e* is the parasitic *e* spoken of on p. 64 (*peiene*); I have noted but one example for *i*, that in Pyramus, *St. Edmond*, line 1459, *serin : lendemain.*

2. CHECKED POSITION. Here interest centres upon the question of the confusion or non-confusion of *ẽn* + consonant with *ãn* + consonant.[2]

The non-confusion of the two has always been commented upon as constituting a characteristic of Anglo-Norman, and as distinguishing it from continental Norman, where the two rapidly assimilated.[3] This distinction between the two sounds is observed by our scribes with a strictness which we would hardly expect of them. The exceptions are very few; they have been cited for Chardri,[4] *Tristran,*[5] and *Boeve.*[6]

11. Ẹ BEFORE L OR R.

Checked *ẹ* + *l* + consonant was early confused with *ę*, as it was generally in checked position. Treatment of it will be found under *ę*, p. 58. Before *r* we must note the forms of the *Camb. Psalt. feorm, enfeorm* (FIRMUS), where the *r* induced an *o* after the *e*.[7]

---

[1] Plahn, p. 5.

[2] For the variants *ẽi* and *ẽie*, see under checked *ę*, p. 58.

[3] Cf. Mall, *Cumpoz*, p. 76; Such. *Auban*, p. 3; Kupferschmidt, Gaimar, p. 417, Grass, *Adam*, p. 141; Vising, *Étude*, p. 69 (*Brandan*), p. 81 (Gaimar), p. 92 (Fantosme).

[4] Koch, p. xxxi.   [5] Vising, *Étude*, p. 14.

[6] Stimming, p. lv. Stimming seems to indicate that *Boeve* is the only poetical text showing the confusion in rhyme in Anglo-Norman; exs. cited by Koch for his text were not called into question by his reviewers, however, and Rottiger, *Der Tristran des Thomas*, Gottingen, 1883, p 30, cites two examples. Rottiger here gives a general bibliography on the point. Suchier, in his *Reimpredigt*, Halle, 1879 (*Bibl. Norman*, I), pp. 69–71, takes up separate exceptions. Cf. his *Grammatik*, p. 69. In *Litblt.* I, 25, he included Fantosme's *Chronique* among the texts showing the confusion, but he corrects the error in *Reimpredigt*, p. 70, f.-n. Stimming, p. 185, gives reference to examples not in rhyme words.   [7] Cf. Such. *Gram.* p. 82.

Ẹ̆

12. FREE Ẹ̆.

A number of interesting points arise in the study of ẹ̆ in Anglo-Norman; we shall consider the following: (1) the reduction of *ie* to *e*, and the confusion of the two in rhyme; (2) the quality of the *e* < *ie*; (3) was *ie* a rising or a falling diphthong? (4) different orthographies found in our texts.

1. IE AND E. We shall include here a similar reduction of *ie* < palatal + *a*. The reduction was cited early in the history of Anglo-Norman studies, as characteristic of the dialect[1] As to the time of the change, we have to distinguish between works in prose and those in poetry; for the latter, again, we must separate the instances in which *e* for *ie* occurs in rhyme words from those in which it appears in the interior of the verse; finally, we should observe the presence and proportion of the rhymes *e* : *e*, *ie* : *ie*, and *ie* . *e*. Only the last illustrates conclusively the Anglo-Norman peculiarity; *e* : *e* would not prove it, for though the *ie* may have been simplified to *e*, it was done before the use of the *e* in rhyme, and might have been caused by reason of analogy or a similar principle. Actual statistics apparently indicate that our poets were not so careless in their use of *ie* and *e* as we might suspect.

In prose texts we find *e* from the beginning of the Anglo-Norman period. Examples have been given for the *Domesday Book*[2] (*Oliver, Cheure < Chieure*); *Oxf. Psalt*[3] (*perre, requer*); *Camb. Psalt.*[4] (seldom, *cel, secle*), *Q. L. R*,[5] etc

For poetry we note the following: Suchier[6] indicates that

---

[1] Cf. Such *Zt.* I, 569; *Français et Provençal*, p. 23, (in) Grober's *Grundriss*, I, 572; *Gram.* pp. 5 and 47, Meyer-Lubke, *Gram.* I, 168, § 173; 173, § 179; 237, § 260, Vising, *Zt.* VI, 381.   [2] *Zt.* VIII, 358-359

[3] Harseim, p. 281, *Zt.* I, 569.   [4] Schumann, p 24.

[5] Schlosser, pp. 3, 22, Plahn, p. 5, the latter gives the proportionate use of *ie* and *e* for *Oxf. Psalt.*, *Camb. Psalt.* and *Q L R.* as follows: *ie* : *e*, *Oxf. Psalt.* 100 : 43; *Camb. Psalt.* 100 . 14, *Q. L. R.* 100 . 26.

[6] *Auban*, p. 3; cf. Uhlemann, p. 588.

ie and *e* were kept separate till after the middle of the twelfth century. About the same date is specified by Meyer,[1] who says that the rhyme *ie* : *e* became more and more frequent in England from the end of the twelfth century. Suchier, in another place,[2] cites examples of the confusion in Philippe de Thaun's *Cumpóz*, though the editor of the *Bestiaire* [3] claims no confusion in his text and restores *ie* in all cases. Philippe's contemporary, the author of the *Brandan*, keeps the two separate.[4] Gaimar, too, observes continental rules,[5] though one may detect a tendency toward the reduction. From the time of Fantosme,[6] in any case, instances of the confusion become abundant, though we may find occasionally a poet who evinces a preference for *e* : *e*, or *ie* . *ie*. We note *ie* : *e* in Angier [7] (here, however, the proportion is in favor of the regular rhymes), in Guillaume de Berneville (examples [8] are given only for *ie* < palatal + *a*), *Boeve*,[9] and *Amadas*.[10]

2. QUALITY OF E < IE. We refer, in the first place, to the remarks on the *e* < A, p. 38. When Meyer first speaks of *e* < *ie*,[11] he gives it as close. Next, Suchier [12] classes this *e* with that < A, as *ẹ*. Paris marks the *e* as *é* in the *Vie St. Gilles*.[13] Meyer [14] seems doubtful of the quality of the *e* and *ie* in his edition of Angier, giving *ié* (*é*), but offering *iè* (*è*) as a substitute, saying there is doubt about it; he attempts no discussion. Stimming [15] specifies *ẹ*.

3. NATURE OF THE DIPHTHONG. As to whether *ie* is a rising or a falling diphthong, the point can be made clearer by comparison with the diphthong *ue* (< ǫ). The two are considered together, p. 71.

---

[1] *Rom.* I, 72   [2] *Gram* p. 47.   [3] Walberg, p. lxxxiv.
[4] Such. *Gram* p. 47.   [5] Vising, *Étude*, p. 86.
[6] *Ibid.* p. 92.   [7] Meyer, p. 194 ; Cloran, p. 47.
[8] p. xxix ; cf. here the corrections of Mussafia, *Rom.* XI, 594, who reduces the number, already small.   [9] Stimming, p. ix.
[10] Andresen, p. 85.   [11] *Rom.* I, 72.   [12] *Zt.* II, 293.
[13] p. xxix.   [14] *Rom.* XII, 194.   [15] *Boeve*, p. ix.

4. ORTHOGRAPHIC VARIANTS OF IE (E).

a. *ee.* The essential facts with regard to this *ee* have already been stated, p. 41. A few references may be given here.[1]

b. *ei.* Examples for this have been noted for the *Bestiaire*[2] and later texts.[3] In the *Apocalypse* I find *teirz*, 405, *ceil*, 515.

c. *eie.* This I have found only in *Arundel Psalt.*,[4] *peiez* (cf. *preiere, creiendrums*). The first *e* seems the parasitic, pretonic *e* described on page 61.

d. *i.* *i* for *ie* occurs frequently : *milz, arire volentirs*, etc. Stimming[5] gives a list of texts showing it. I find it often in *Otinel* and *Aspremont*, both in the interior and at the end of verses : *tirz*, 128 (cf. *Olivirs*, 58, *chevalirs*, 72, *premir*, 74, etc.), also in the *Fabliau du Héron, mestir, rivire*,[6] etc.

13. CHECKED Ẹ.

The confusion of *ẹ* with *ę* in checked position has already been commented upon, cf. p. 53. The variant *ei* occurs for *ę*, too, in *seit* (SEPTEM), Gaimar.[7] In addition we note *ae* and *ea* which appear as variants of *ę* alone ; *ae* occurs often in the *Dialogues* of Gregory[8] (*apraes, engraes, daestre*), *Auban*, *saet* (SEPTEM), *Pèlerinage, bael*, 216. In Ms L. of the *Alexis* we find *seat* (SEPTEM), which is a borrowing from middle English.[9]

14. Ẹ BEFORE A PALATAL.

Here we find for the most part *i*, though not infrequently *ei* (*preise* for *prise*). With regard to the *ei* there is a question whether it is a mere graphic variant of *i*, or whether it represents a sound other than *i*. Stimming gives examples;[10]

[1] Mall, *Cumpoz*, p 68 ; Meyer-Lubke, *Gram* I, 173, § 179 ; Such. *Gram* p. 48 , Stimming, *Boeve*, p. 202.   [2] Walberg, p lxxxiv.

[3] Stimming, *Boeve*, p 202   [4] *Zt* XI, 530 ; XII, 6, 45.

[5] *Boeve*, p 202.   [6] *Rom.* XXVI, 88.

[7] Stimming, *Boeve*, p. 175.   [8] Cloran, p. 47.

[9] Such. *Zt.* XIX, 81, f.-n. 10, *Gram* p. 42. See also under *a +* palatal, p. 40.   [10] *Boeve*, p. 187.

we may add those taken from the *Oxf. Psalt. (neie)*, *Camb. Psalt.* and *Vie St. Gilles.*[1] In the latter text words in which ẹ + palatal occur are not found in rhymes in *i*, so that Paris hesitates to say if De Berneville used *iei, ie, ei, e,* or *i*. Vising, in his review,[2] says such a state of affairs is the result of a coincidence, and that the regular Anglo-Norman product was *i*.

15. Ẹ BEFORE A NASAL.

1. FREE POSITION. Here we find *ie* and *e* as in the case of ẹ + simple oral consonant, but we must remember that in Anglo-Norman the continental *ie* before a nasal does not suffer the reduction to *e* as frequently as it does when before an oral consonant.

a Orthographic variants (*ee, ei, i, eie, iei*). Stimming[3] gives texts showing these. In *Otinel* we note *bin (bien)* 123, and *veint (vient)* 227, the latter also in the *Apocalypse*, 83, 137. The *Brandan veient*[4] is another example of the parasitic pretonic *e* (cf. p. 61). An example of *iei* is furnished by *Camb. Psalt. mieins*, XVII, 34.

2. CHECKED POSITION.

a. Variants (*ei, eie*). The variant *ei* occurs for both ẹ and ę in checked position (cf. p. 57), *dedeins, leins, veint*. A further variant of the *ei* arises from the addition to it of the parasitic post-tonic *e*, as *seyens* (ECCE INTUS). Cf. *eyens* (ANTEA) and *leyens* (ILLAC INTUS).[5]

16. Ẹ (AND Ę) BEFORE L.

We have already referred (p. 54) to the confusion of ẹ with ę when before *l*, the *l* having a tendency to keep an open vowel (cf. *a + l*, p. 48). The history of the vowel before the *l* must, of course, go hand in hand with that of the *l* itself, which remains, for the most part, in our earliest texts, though the tendency to vocalization ($> u$) is to be

---

[1] Harseim, p. 282 ; Schumann, p. 25 ; Paris, p. xxx.
[2] *Litblt.* IV, 311.   [3] Stimming, *Boeve*, p. 203.
[4] Hammer, p. 91.   [5] Stimming, *Boeve*, pp. 180 and 185.

noted at a very early date (cf. p. 87). Again, where the *l* is kept, we have to distinguish between the cases in which we find the glide *a* (*-eal*) or simple *-el*. Philippe de Thaun did not know of *-eal* < *-EL* (according to his two editors [1]), though Suchier [2] cites *eals, ceals* from the *Cumpoz* (L.). The *Oxf. Psalt.* has, as a rule, *-el* (*oisels*), *-eal* occurring exceptionally [3] (*chalemeals*). In *Camb Psalt.* [4] *-eal* is not infrequent, and *-eols* occurs too. *Oxf. Roland* [5] has *-els*, except in one instance (*healmes*). The *Q. L. R.* [6] has *-els* almost without exception (*beaus* once). In the *Brandan* we find (by the side of older forms) *oiseus, beus*, etc. [7] This *-eus* (without the glide) is found in Norman and Anglo-Norman texts, seldom elsewhere in Northern French [8] After the time of the early texts the combination *e* + *l* + consonant is represented in many different ways, older and later forms being used without apparent discrimination. As a rule we may say that the normal Anglo-Norman form was *-eals, -eaus*.

1. VARIANTS. We have to record the following variants.

a. *eus, us*   *eus* has just been cited from *Brandan;* examples occur in *Vie St. Thomas* (as II, 47, *beu sire*) and *Boeve.* [9] The *-us* is probably a development from *-eus* (cf. *-eol* > *-ol, eal* > *al*), and occurs only in later texts. To Stimming's list [10] we may add *Apocalypse chevus*, 52, 452.

b. *als, aus.* These may be reductions from *-eals, -eaus.* In *Camb. Psalt.* we find *ruissals*, [11] *nenal, oal*, in *Q. L. R.*, *halme.* [12] We note *haume* in *Lois Guillaume*, [13] *oisaus* in *Bestiaire* and Angier [14]

c. *eols, eous, ols, ous.* *Iceols* is found in *Camb. Psalt* and *Brandan* The *o* in *iceols* is doubtless a glide (like the *a* in *-eals*); *-ols* is a development from *eols*; in the *Camb. Psalt.*

[1] Mall, p. 65; Walberg, p xlii.
[2] *Gram.* p. 82   [3] Harseim, p. 282.   [4] Schumann, p. 23.
[5] Forster, *Zt* I, 565   [6] Schlosser, p 21.   [7] *Zt.* I, 565.
[8] Such *Gram* p 81; Meyer-Lubke, *Gram.* I, 163, § 163
[9] Stimming, p. 174.   [10] *Boeve*, p 175   [11] Schumann, p. 23.
[12] Schlosser, p. 21.   [13] Matzke, p xlvi.   [14] Such *Gram.* p. 81.

we note *chevols* (XXXIX, 15, LXVIII, 5) which is of not
infrequent occurrence; Gaimar has *ous* (ILLOS).[1]

d. *oels, ouls, euls.* In the *Arundel Psalt.* we have a number of variants, some of which are not found among the above.
We note: *icoels*,[2] *ouls* (*couls, icouls*, common),[3] *euls*,[4] *els, eols, ols.*[5]

17. PRETONIC E. (Here we have no occasion to distinguish between close and open *e.*)

1. FALL OF PRETONIC E.

a. Before a vowel. The early fall of pretonic hiatus *e* in
Anglo-Norman is always spoken of [6] as characteristic of that
dialect as compared with French of the continent. We
have to include here ending accented forms of preterites
(like *eümes*) or imperfect subjunctives (like *eust*) which originally had pretonic *o* in place of the *e* (*oïmes, oust*); [7] in the
Q. L. R., for example, we find *oust* (monosyllable), *eüst*, and
ust. We must take account also of the peculiarly Anglo-
Norman contraction illustrated in *lele* for *leale*, which has
already been referred to on page 49 (pretonic *a*).

In the *Cumpoz* and *Oxf. Psalt.* we find the *e* retained,
though in the verb forms referred to the *o* has weakened
to *e*. The *Lois Guillaume* keeps this *o* consistently (*oust,
poust*, etc.).[8] The *Camb. Psalt.* and Q. L. R. show the fall,
while the *Brandan* and Gaimar [9] retain the *e*. After the
time of Fantosme the fall becomes frequent; we may say,
therefore, that even in Anglo-Norman the poets do not regularly elide the *e* previous to the thirteenth century.[10]

---

[1] Such. *Gram.* p 82; Stimming, *Boeve*, p. 175.   [2] *Zt.* XI, 516.
[3] *Ibid.* XI, 520, 524; XII, 4, 14, 22.   [4] *Ibid.* XII, 14.   [5] *Ibid.* XII, 1.
[6] Cf. for example, *Rom.* I, 71; XXV, 531; *Zt.* I, 569, IV, 419; Meyer-
Lubke, *Gram.* I, 319, § 377; Stimming, *Boeve*, pp. xxxiii and 178.
[7] These forms were made the object of especial study by Suchier,
Auban, p. 27. Paris summarizes Suchier's results and gives the best
general statement for the whole phenomenon, in his *Gme. de Berneville*,
p. xxii.   [8] Such. *Litblt.* XXII, 121.   [9] Cf. Vising, *Étude*, p. 82.
[10] Cf. Meyer, *Vie St. Thomas*, p. xxix. Meyer believes the *e* is not
to be elided in his text.

b. Before a consonant. The fall of the *e* here is even more characteristically Anglo-Norman than that of the pretonic *e* in hiatus; the loss of the latter *e* becomes general on the Continent too, but that of pretonic *e* before a consonant does not.[1] For convenience of observation, we may divide the examples according as they show the combination consonant + *e* + consonant, or vowel + *e* + consonant. In the former case the second consonant is usually *r*, and instances are to be drawn mostly from futures and conditionals (*frai, frei, trouvrai, durrai*), though examples furnished by other words are not lacking (as *vigrous, pelrin,* and the like).[2] For vowel + *e* + consonant we note the following: Suchier[3] speaks of *seira* (< *seiera*) as one of the Anglo-Norman marks of the *Oxf. Psalt.* The same fall of the *e* occurs in *Q. L. R.* in seven futures (*enveirai = enveierai*) by the side of twenty-five which keep the *e*.[4] Stimming[5] gives further examples, like *espuntez = espuentez*. The examples here are illustrations of the fall of the protonic syllable, and are, of course, to be noted in connection with the similar fall of the post-tonic *e* after vowels (cf. p. 63).

2. PARASITIC PRETONIC E. The insertion of an *e* where it does not belong etymologically takes place under the same conditions as those for which we have just noted its loss; in fact, this process seems more frequent than the loss of the *e*. It is not characteristically Anglo-Norman, though very usual there. Stimming treats of this point at length.[6] The svarabhactic *e* appears often in futures and conditionals, and words in general where one of a group of consonants is *r*, *perderez, ferete* (cf. *averil, Otinel,* 46), though a few examples occur for other consonants, as *sabeloun, jovene.* The *e* sometimes acquires such a value as to have other vowels substituted for it, as: *ferté > fereté > ferité ; perdrai > per-*

---

[1] Cf. Such. *Auban,* pp. 33 and 40 ; Paris, *Rom* XXV, 532.
[2] Cf. Schlosser, *Q. L R.* p. 4 ; Hammer, *Zt.* IX, 85 ; Stimming, *Boeve,* p. 178.   [3] *Zt.* I, 569.   [4] Meiwart, p. 10.
[5] *Boeve,* p. 178.   [6] *Ibid.* pp 179–181.

derai > *perdurai* (cf. *perle* > *pérele* > *peréle*, p. 64). Stimming considers apart from the cases just considered those in which the parasitic *e* appears before or after vowels and diphthongs, as *perdeu* (*perdu*), *deeyns* (DE INTUS), *meit* (MISIT), *seonge*. Such words call for various explanations ; as, analogy, mistakes of scribes, and the like. Doubtless a similar group of examples is to be added here, made up of words in which the pretonic parasitic *e* precedes the diphthong *ie*, as *peiez*, (*pieds*), *veient* (*vient*), etc. Cf. pp. 57 and 58.

3. PRETONIC E BEFORE A NASAL. Here we need only refer to Stimming, [1] he distinguishes cases in which the *e* occurs before a single consonant from those in which it is found before several. In either case *e* interchanges with *a*, and Stimming says that such is the case particularly when *e* precedes a single nasal consonant. It may be questioned whether this statement will hold good, if we take from the list of examples of *e* before single *n* the many forms of (*menacer* >) *manacer*, where the *a* dates back to Popular Latin times.[2] *am* — (*an* —) occurs often in *Alexis*, as *ampairet*, L, 2, e, *amfant*, L, 5, b. In *Arundel Psalt.* we note *anemis*.[3] It seems very probable that the *a* merely reflects the general Anglo-Norman fondness for pretonic *a* already spoken of on p. 49 and referred to again in our next paragraph.

4. VARIANTS OF PRETONIC E.

a. Phonetic (*a, i, o, u*) We here have to refer, in the first place, to our note on pretonic *a* (p. 49, § 6, 2, a). Our dialect has a distinct predilection for *a* in this position, original *a* being sometimes kept (*chavaler*), or else supplanting etymological *e* (*ascient*). Stimming [4] gives examples of the other variants, *i, o, u*, —, which are to be explained usually by assimilation, attraction, and the like. To his instances of *u* we may add *dumurez* (*Auban*),[5] *Nuvers, espuruns* (*Amadas et Ydoine*),[6] *jutas, jutiez* (*getter*) from the *Arundel Psalt.*[7]

---

[1] *Boeve*, p. 185.   [2] Cf. Nyrop, *Gram.* I, 15, § 12.

[3] *Zt.* XII, 55.   [4] *Boeve*, p. 177.   [5] *Zt.* II, 343

[6] *Ibid.* XIII, 86.   [7] *Ibid.* XII, 51, 53.

and *jutta* from one of the latest texts, the *Apocalypse,* 1099. For *i* we find *chivaus, chimin,* etc.; for *o, solum, bosoyne,* etc.

b. Orthographic (*eo, ae, oe*). The *eo,* which we have already recorded (pp. 43 and 53) as a variant of accented *e,* occurs for *e* in pretonic position too, though not frequently; to Stimming's examples [1] should be added the *enfeormethe* of the *Camb. Psalt.*[2] We may mention *ae* also which is of frequent occurrence in the *Arundel Psalt.; meslaescerai, baealtet,*[3] and noted by Schlosser [4] for the *Q. L. R. raegnad.* Schumann [5] gives *oe,* as distinguished from *ae,* for the *Camb. Psalt. estoerat, portoeras,* etc.

18 POST-TONIC E.

1. FALL OF POST-TONIC E.

a After vowels.[6] The loss of the *e* after vowels has been cited as characteristic of our dialect since the time of the earliest studies on the dialect In the very first number of *Romania,* Meyer calls attention to it This loss swells to a notable extent the total of irregularities in Anglo-Norman, since it brings about the confusion of *ee · e* in participles or substantives; it is responsible for feminine possessives like *mei, tu* (cf. p 118), and of imperfect endings *-eint* (for *-eient,* cf p 124). As to the time of the fall, all agree that it took place earlier in Anglo-Norman than on the continent; we may place it in the course of the twelfth century. The *Brandan* is the first poetical text with which the phenomenon is usually associated. Stimming [7] gives a list of texts and examples. We may add from the *Arundel Psalt.* im-

---

[1] *Boeve,* p 178   [2] Such. *Gram* p 82.
[3] *Zt* XI, 521 , XII, 16   [4] p. 37   [5] p 27.
[6] The general bibliography on this point is the following· *Rom* I, 71 ; Such. *Auban,* p 5; Koschwitz, *Zt* II, 482 ; Vising, *Étude,* p. 70 , *Litblt* IV, 311 , Meyer-Lubke, *Gram* I, 261, § 305 ; 290, § 640 (*glori, estudi,* etc); Stimming, *Boeve,* p 1 (effect on metie), Nyrop, *Gram* I, 210. For later Anglo-Norman, cf. Meyer, *Bozon,* p lx.
[7] *Boeve,* p 182.

perfect forms like *criou, humiliou;*[1] in *Amadas et Ydoine*[2] we note *rai* : *saie, pasme* : *pasmee.*

b. After consonants. The loss of the *e* here, too, is considered an Anglo-Norman peculiarity. It is by no means as early as that after vowels, and becomes frequent only toward the end of the thirteenth century. Suchier studies this point in detail[3] and concludes that the fall of *e* was gradual, taking place first (and mostly) after *r* (already in *Arundel Psalt.*[4] we note *sir*), next after *l* (*nul = nule*), finally after *m* or *n* (*dam, un = dame, une*).

2. PARASITIC POST-TONIC E. Since, as we have just seen, the *e* fell in so many cases, and with no apparent consistency, we may readily conceive of the state of uncertainty among our scribes as to its proper use and proper omission; we find numbers of cases where the post-tonic *e* is added with no etymological right. Stimming speaks of these at length;[5] examples are *nule* (masc.), *foreste,* and the curious instances where the *e* is inserted between a stem and a flexional *s* as *prest(e)s, coup(e)s,* — this being just the contrary of the cases where an *e* with an etymological background is omitted, as *tuz* (= TOTAS), *veys* (= VIAS), *seys* (= SIAS), and the like. We may add some examples from the *Arundel Psalt.* where we find the masculine participles *tresturnee, eslevee;*[6] *meismee,*[7] and *jures* (= *jours*).[8] The parasitic *e* may have other vowels substituted for it: as *i* (*pans > panes >) panis,* (*fins > fines >) finis;* and *u* (*meilurs > meilures >) meilurus* (*Boeve*[9]). Cf. below (3, orthographic variants)..

In the *Apocalypse* we note a remarkable perversion in the example furnished by the rhyme *perele* : *cristele* (line 1297), where the stages were *pérle > pérele > peréle* (cf. p. 61 and

---

[1] *Zt.* XII, 19, 26.   [2] *Ibid.* XIII, 86.   [3] *Auban,* pp. 36–39.
[4] *Zt.* XII, 7. Cf. also the rhymes cited by Meyer, *Rom.* XXV, 255 : *pere* : *primer, Pol* : *paroles, cors* : *paroles* from *Descente St. Paul.*
[5] *Boeve,* pp. 182–183.   [6] *Zt.* XI, 519 ; XII, 31.
[7] *Ibid.* XII, 23.   [8] *Ibid.* XII, 2.   [9] Stimming, p. 184.

under the consonant *r*).   In the same text, line 477, we note
foiez (= *fois*).

3. ORTHOGRAPHIC VARIANTS (*i, u, a, oe, ae*).   These are
given by Stimming[1] as follows: *i, meu, -istis, -int.*   (This *i*
occurs with great frequency in *Arundel Psalt.: chosis, eglisis,
taisis, vindrint* [2]); *u, trovunt; a, ora.*   (This *a* for *e* occurs
in nearly every strophe of *Alexis* L, as *nostra*, strophe 3;
tendra, 24; *lungament*, 69; *anames*, 122, etc.)   We may add
also the *oe* of the *Camb. Psalt* cited by Schumann,[3] *terroe,
palmoes.*   In the printed edition (Michel) we find *oe* in the
last few psalms only; elsewhere *ae*, as *suflae*, XXV, 2;
fuiaent, XXX, 12, etc. (many cases).   In the *Arundel Psalt.*
too, we note *ae: terrae.*[4]

I

19. I, TONIC

There is little of importance to note here, and I shall
merely make reference to several points treated by Stimming.   These are the rhyming of *i : e* ;[5] *i: u* (cf. p. 79, § 32);
comparative use of *y* and *i* by scribes; [6] nothing especial
arises in the consideration of *i* before a nasal.[7]   As varying
orthographies of *i* we find *e* (*esgles* = *église*), *ei* (*conqueis*),[8]
ie (*fiez;* cf. below, § 20), and we may add the *u* of the *Q. L. R.
afuble* < *affibula.*[9]

20. I, ATONIC

Here we may add to the two variants given by Stim-
ming; [10] that is, *e* (*dener*) and *ei* (*deiables*), three others . *ai* of
Camb. Psalt. LXXIII, 14, *daiables* (cf. CIII, 26, *daible*); *oi*
of *Arundel Psalt., foiede,*[11] and *ie* of *Vie Gregoire*, line 1867,
dierrai = *dirrai.*

[1] *Boeve*, pp 183, 184.   [2] *Zt.* XI, 528, XII, 12, 14, 47.
[3] p. 27   [4] *Zt.* XII, 10.
[5] *Boeve*, pp. lv, 188.   [6] *Ibid.* p. 186.
[7] *Boeve*, p. 188.   [8] *Ibid.* p. 187
[9] Such. *Gram.* § 11, *a*, 5.   [10] *Boeve*, p. 188.   [11] *Zt.* XII, 14.

F

$\overset{\text{o}}{\text{Q}}$

21. TONIC Q.

So far as results, noted in rhymes or orthography, are concerned, we do not have to observe a distinction between free and checked tonic ϱ (except in the case of *eu* which occurs but seldom, cf. below, p. 68, 3). Our first poetical text, *Cumpoz* (L), shows a distinct preference for keeping original *o* in the orthography, and even substitutes the *o* for etymological $u < \bar{u}$ (though the examples given [1] are mostly for *u* in pretonic position): *jogier*, *mors*, etc. In *Brandan*, too, we have a similar state of affairs,[2] and at a later time, in Angier,[3] Chardri, and *Adam*,[4] we note a tendency to keep *o*. I record this fact only for the sake of historical completeness; the really important feature in connection with ϱ is treated in our next paragraph.

1. U AND O. a. We find *u* written for *o* in our earliest texts. In fact, such a use must be very old, though we cannot accept, in its entirety, the reasoning of Lucking,[5] at least in so far as it concerns Anglo-Norman. He argues that the writing of *u* for *o* must have preceded the time when $u \ (< \bar{u})$ began to have the value of *u*, since after it signified that value, scribes would not think of using it to designate still another sound (that of the $u < $ o). The use of *u* for *o* is likewise to be found on the continent, but it seems to have been favored nowhere as it was in Anglo-Norman.[6] No difficulty attaches to the appearance of *u* for *o* in prose or in the interior of verse. We find *u* in the *Cumpoz*,[7] in the *Lois Guillaume*[8] (here *o* is found in only one word), in *Oxf. Psalt.*,[9] *Camb. Psalt.*,[10] and *Q. L. R.*[11]

b. We have to consider, however, that in some poetical

---

[1] Mall, p. 41.   [2] Hammer, p. 87.
[3] Moyer, p. 197.   [4] Stimming, *Boeve*, p. 190.
[5] *Die Aeltesten Französischen Mundarten*, Berlin, 1877, p. 149.
[6] Such *Gram.* p. 14.   [7] Mall, pp. 41, 46, 47.   [8] Matzke, p. xlvii.
[9] Harseim, p. 294.   [10] Schumann, p. 40.   [11] Schlosser, p. 49.

texts this u, as used for o, rhymes with $u < \bar{u}$; that is, with
the u which in Île-de-France had the value of $\ddot{u}$. The best
statements for this phenomenon are those of Suchier.[1] In
the number of the *Literaturblatt* cited he gives a detailed
list of ten texts which keep the two u's ($< o$ and $< \bar{u}$) separate in rhyme and eight having the two confused. These
numbers should be nine and nine, since Angier rhymes the
two;[2] such a usage by Angier is all the more remarkable
since, at best, he uses u for o but seldom, even in the interior of the verse.[3] Several other texts are to be added to the
number of those illustrating the confusion in rhyme In
Vie St. Thomas[4] we note *ure* (HORAM) : *aventure*, *muz*
(MŪTUS) : *tuz*. Stimming records the same license for
Boeve,[5] and in the Bible *Fragment* we see *natu1e* : *ure* (607),
hume : *amertume* (609).

Suchier counts the confusion as characteristic of North
Anglo-Norman as compared with the Southern district As
to the pronunciation of the two u's thus made to rhyme
together, we can suppose only that both were equivalent to
Latin $\bar{u}$ (French *ou*) in pronunciation. Suchier specifies $\ddot{u}$,
Meyer-Lübke, u. I append some references on this point[6]

2. Ou.[7] *ou* was not popular in early Anglo-Norman, and
in our first texts the examples are to be counted by ones
and twos, the oldest instance is *Cumpoz* (L) 3305, *pente-
couste*. Continental influence probably induced the use of
the *ou* where found.[8] Angier evinces special fondness for

[1] *Auban*, p. 5 (cf. *Zt.* II, 313), *Litblt.* IX, 176.

[2] This is Suchier's own correction , *Gram.* p 12, c.

[3] Meyer, p 197 , Cloran, p 47.   [4] Introd p xxviii.

[5] p. lvii.   The reference on line 8 of this page is to v. 1163, and
not 1193.

[6] Meyer-Lübke, *Gram.* I, 73, § 48 ; Mall, *Cump* p. 47 , Walberg, *Best.*
p xlvi; Uhlem. *Aub.* p. 569; Nyrop, *Gram* I, 166; Vising, *Étude*,
p 72 , Rottiger, *Tristran*, p 37 , Grass, *Adam*, p 121. (Here is a
general review of the subject.)

[7] See Such. *Gram.* p. 15 (and his correction with regard to *Q L. R*
on p. 88), Stim. *Boeve*, p. 190   [8] Meyer-Lübke, *Gram.* I, 141, § 133.

ou, alternating it with *o* (cf. p. 67), but preferring it for finals in -osus.[1]

3. EU.[2] We find only isolated cases of *eu* in Anglo-Norman; Chardri, *pleurent;* [3] *Auban, piteus;* [4] and a few in *Boeve,*[5] as *neveu, pecheurs*, may be added to the instances Suchier cites (cf. below, p. 72, 3).

4. ORTHOGRAPHIC VARIANT OF U. The variant to be noted here, *ui*, arises as follows: etymological *ui* ($<$ ŭ, ō, ŏ $+$ palatal) is often reduced to *u* in Anglo-Norman (cf. p. 80). Scribes, in their blundering attempts to be correct, not only restore this *u* (from etymological *ui*) to *ui*, but replace other *u*'s (in this instance *u* which is $<$ ǫ) with *ui*; the adjective *tut* is often rendered by *tuit* in this way; to Stimming's examples[6] we may add *Arundel Psalt., tuitte terre, tuit tuen sacrifise,*[7] and *Dialog. Greg.*[8]

22. Q BEFORE A PALATAL.

1. OI AND O. The *o* of *oi* was originally close *o*, as in general French, though English words like *cross* and *voice* show that Anglo-Norman knew open *o* too; *cross* is an example of the reduction of ǫi to ǫ; *vǫiz* seems to occur in our earliest texts.

2. UI AND U. The *ui*, which is the rule in our earliest texts, reflects the original ǫi; it is to be seen in *Cumpoz,*[9] *Oxf. Psalt.,*[10] *Camb. Psalt.,*[11] *Q. L. R.,*[12] etc. In *Auban* we find the writing *oui.*[13] There are but few instances of the reduction of *ui* (for *oi*) to *u*. Stimming[14] cites, for example, *cruz, angusse*, and (perhaps) *conu.*

---

[1] Meyer, p. 197.
[2] See Such. *Gram.* pp. 29 and 31.
[3] *Zt.* III, 593.
[4] Uhlemann, p. 569.
[5] Stimming, p. 190.
[6] *Boeve*, p. 190.
[7] *Zt.* XII, 46, 2.
[8] Cloran, p. 48.
[9] Mall, pp. 60, 61, 63, 65.
[10] Harseim, p. 296.
[11] Schumann, p. 42.
[12] Schlosser, p. 51.
[13] Uhlemann, p. 586.
[14] *Boeve*, p. 205.

23. Q BEFORE A NASAL.

Before a nasal there is no distinction, so far as results are concerned, among free ǫ, checked ǫ, free ǫ (in those cases in which it does not diphthongize, for whatever reason) and checked ǫ, as all rhyme together. Texts are mentioned by Stimming;[1] add the *Bestiaire*,[2] and in *Vie Gregoire*, line 1683, we note *om : region* (cf. *Cumpoz*, line 251, *hume : nune*).

1. ON AND UN. a. We find the same interchange of *o* and *u* here as in the case of oral consonants, but the proportion is different; before a nasal, *u* is used, almost to the exclusion of *o* in orthography, even by Angier,[3] who otherwise favors *o* or *ou* (cf. p. 67). We refer here to *Liber Censualis*,[4] *Oxf. Psalt.*,[5] *Camb. Psalt.*,[6] *Amadas*,[7] *Auban*,[8] etc. *Boeve* forms the exception, since *on* is there preferred.[9]

b. The *u* (< ǫ + nasal) may rhyme with *u* < *ū* + nasal as the two *u*'s do before oral consonants. In fact, the first examples for the rhyming of the two are when they precede nasals, and not orals. These examples are *Brandan, uns : compaignuns*,[10] Gaimar, *un : incarnaciun*.[11]

2. OUN. This is not a development to be compared with that of *a* + nasal > *aun*. The *ou*, as used before nasals, is doubtless an extension of the *ou* already spoken of (p. 67, § 21, 2), which was borrowed from Continental French. Koschwitz[12] made a study of the point, and indicates that the development may have been *o* > *ou* > *u*. Our texts, however, do not substantiate this theory; *ou* appeared at a comparatively late date. The first example I have noticed is that in Chardri,[13] Ms. V (thirteenth to fourteenth century, cf. p. 22); a few occur in *Boeve*[14] (*ount, vount, fount*) and *Auban*.[15]

---

[1] *Boeve*, p liii.   [2] Walberg, p. xlvi.   [3] Cloran, p. 48.
[4] *Zt.* VIII, 358.   [5] Harseim, p. 295   [6] Schumann, p. 41.
[7] Andresen, p. 86.   [8] Uhlemann, p 575.   [9] Stimming, p. 191.
[10] Koschwitz, *Zt.* II, 343.   [11] Kupferschmidt, p. 417.
[12] *Ueberlieferung*, p. 32 ss.   [13] Koch, p. xxxi.
[14] Stimming, p. 192.   [15] Uhlemann, p. 569.

Q̧

The definite history of many of the phenomena arising in a study of ǫ in Anglo-Norman is yet to be written. One cannot read what has been proposed and then, after an observation of the examples for himself, be satisfied that the last word has been said. I offer some fragmentary suggestions on various points, hoping thereby to invite attention to and discussion of them. A final solution demands a careful and detailed study of ǫ in all the texts; such a study will surely bear fruit.[1]

24. O, UE, EU, U, AND E.

1. O. The keeping of *o* in the undiphthongized (by the side of the diphthongized) form is characteristic of Anglo-Norman. We find *o* in our older texts, though not with consistent frequency; for example, in *Cumpoz*[2] and *Bestiaire;*[3] in *Lois Guillaume*[4] (*pople, pot, quor*, etc.), to the entire exclusion of *ue* or *oe;* in the *Psalters o* is found, though not in the majority of cases[5] (in *Arundel Psalt.* we note *quor*[6]), while in the *Q. L. R. o* prevails in the proportion of four to one.[7] We refer to examples of *o* in later texts, as follows: Angier,[8] Chardri,[9] Gme. de Berneville,[10] and *Amadas.*[11] (For *oi* < ǫ + palatal, cf. below, p. 80, § 33, 2.)

2. UE. This is not the place to enter upon, or even to refer to, the extensive bibliography of the interesting general questions as to the history of the diphthongs *ue* < ǫ and

---

[1] The points following may be found, amplified in some cases, in an article in *Mod. Lang. Notes,* XVIII, 106–111.

[2] Mall, pp. 47, 48.　　　　　[3] Walberg, p. lxxxv.

[4] Matzke, p. xlvii.　　　　　[5] Harseim, p 292 ; Schumann, p. 33.

[6] *Zt.* XI, 524, 525, 526 ; XII, 16.

[7] Plahn, p. 5.　　　　　[8] Meyer, p 196 ; Cloran, p. 48.

[9] Koch, p. xxviii (cf. *Zt.* III, 593).　　　[10] Paris, p. xxxi.

[11] *Zt.* XIII, 85. For a general statement, cf. Such. *Gram.* p. 41.

ie < ȩ (on p 56 we referred to the present section for a consideration of the latter) : whether the *u* of *ue* was pronounced *ou* or *u*; whether the diphthong was rising or falling; when the pronunciation *o* (Mod. Fr. *eu*) came in, and the like. This latter point is particularly difficult to decide for Anglo-Norman, both on account of the great confusion of orthographies, and because the *eu* to which we are accustomed in French texts of the continent is extremely rare in Anglo-Norman (cf. just below, no. 3). We have reason to suppose that, for a time at least, *ue* had a double value in Anglo-Norman, that is, *u-e* and *o*.[1] The earliest text for which I note the pronunciation *ò* claimed for *ue* is Chardri [2] (There is evidence, however, that the sound *o* existed earlier; cf below, 6, *e*.)

As to whether *ue* and *ie* were rising or falling diphthongs it is difficult to discover essential facts on which to base conclusions. We have already seen (p. 55) that *e* for *ie* is a leading Anglo-Norman characteristic; this, of course, points to a pronunciation *ié*. We shall see below (no 4) that *u* occurs for *ue*; this points to a pronunciation *úe*. The *Oxf. Psal*, where we find marks of accentuation, renders *ie* by *ié*, *ue* by both *úe* and *ué* It seems as if the stress must have varied at different periods of the language, or with different scribes or in some other (unknown) way, such was obviously the case in our dialect where we have *ue*, *u*, *e*; *ie*, *i*, *e*; theorists on the original nature or state of these diphthongs must seek their data outside of Anglo-Norman lines.[3]

An important point to be observed with regard to *ue* in Anglo-Norman is that it may rhyme with ȩ, and thus give rise to a set of rhymes whose exact parallel is not to be found on the continent; such rhymes are *quer: honurer*,

---

[1] Koschwitz, *Ueberlieferung*, pp. 29, 73.

[2] Koch, p. xxviii

[3] For general remarks here, cf. Suchier, *Zt.* I, 291 ; *Gram.* pp. 40 and 48 ; Nyrop, *Litblt.* I, 223.

chanter, counter. They are to be found in *Auban, Donnei,*
Bozon, and other texts.[1]

3. EU. We have already referred to the rarity of *eu* for
ǫ (§ 21, 3), and we shall have to record still fewer cases of
eu for (*ue*) ǫ. Stimming[2] gives *seut, veut* (in which, however,
the *u* may represent an *l* which has vocalized), *queur, peuple,
veulle, peut, demeure.* [*demeure* should not be included here,
as its *o* was ǫ.[3]] We have to study separately each word
and text to determine approximately the phonetic value of
the *eu.* For the *Vie Thomas,* for example, Meyer[4] assigns
different values to the *eu,* according as it represents general
French *ue* (*veut*) or ǫ (*eurent = orent*).

4. U. *u,* representing ǫ, has always been recognized as a
marked Anglo-Norman characteristic; it is found in Philippe,
Oxf. Psalt., Q. L. R., and *Brandan,* among our earlier texts:
buf, put, vult, uvrent, etc.[5] Our dialect is apparently the
only one in which we find an ǫ represented by an *u.* However, if we look upon the *u* as a reduction of the diphthong
ue, and not as a variant of undiphthongized ǫ, there is nothing striking about the *u.* In the earlier stages of Anglo-
Norman studies the *u* was treated as such a variant of ǫ,[6]
and this might seem natural enough in view of the fact of
the Anglo-Norman fondness for keeping the ǫ (cf. p. 70,
§ 24, 1), which is itself a distinct peculiarity. Considering,
however, what we have already said as to the breaking up
of the diphthongs *ue* and *ie* into *u, e* and *i, e,* it seems more

---

[1] Cf. Sturzinger, *Orth. Gall.* p. 46 ; Paris, *Rom.* XXV, 532 ; Meyer,
Bozon, p. lix, 3.   [2] *Boeve,* p. 208.

[3] Cf. *Zt.* II, 509 and Paris, *Gme. de Berneville,* p. xxxi, foot-note 1.
Stimming gave *demeur* under ǫ on p. 190. On p. 208 he is citing from
Stürzinger, who (wrongly) gives ǫ.

[4] Introd. p. xxix. Cf. *touz : leus* (LŎCUM), Apoc. l. 309.

[5] Cf. Grober, *Zt.* II, 509 ; Meyer-Lübke, *Gram.* I, 202, § 217 ; Such.
Français et Provençal, p. 23, (in) Gröber's *Grundriss,* I, 572 ; *Gram.*
p. 41 ; Stim. *Boeve,* p. 208.

[6] Cf. for example, Mall. *Cumpoz,* p. 50 ; Fichte, *Camb. Psalt.* p. 63 ;
Zt. II, 481.

probable, to the present writer, that the *u* in question is out
of *ue*. I know of no suggestion that *i* (for *ie* < ę) is a variant of ę, and yet the history of *ie* and *ue* must have been
the same in many particulars. It seems to me that to claim,
even in Anglo-Norman (where I admit all kinds of irregularities), an *u* for a free tonic ǫ before oral consonants, is
going too far. With *ue* so constant a product in general
French and in Anglo-Norman, too, explanations of any
phase of the history of ǫ that do not take *ue* into account,
where possible, are hazardous. Surely, when we confront
vult with *vuelt*, it is more reasonable to suppose *vult* a later
form of *vuelt* than to think that, with no apparent reason, ǫ
went two different ways, becoming *u* in *vult*, diphthongizing
in *vuelt*.

There are cases in which the *ue* can have played no part,
and where we have evident confusion, or interchange, of
orthographies by the scribes. These are given by Stimming:[1] *vult* (VOLUIT), *nus* (NOSTER), etc., and the imperfect
endings *-ue*, *-ut*, for *-oe*, *-oue*. (Cf. below, p. 123, § 64, 1.)

5. E. *e* for *ue* is said to be characteristically Anglo-
Norman, too. There is little specific discussion on the time
difference between the *e* and the *u* as used for *ue*. Meyer-
Lübke[2] treats of *ue* > *e* first, saying that it occurs early,
then goes on to say, "One is surprised to find *u* also for *ue*,"
as if *e* were the more characteristic or usual Stimming[3]
says *ue* > ę, especially after the year 1200. If what I have
said above (No. 4) as to the derivation of *u* from *ue* is correct, it follows that I must consider the original accentuation
of the diphthong to have been *úe*, and therefore any time
difference must be in favor of *u* as older than *e*. Any such
difference in Anglo-Norman is merely relative, and we need
not suppose that *u* was used regularly for a period of years
and that afterward *e* came in; the difference was doubtless
slight, and the use of the one or the other depended on the

---

[1] *Boeve*, p. 189. Cf. *voult* in *Vie St. Edmond*, l. 454.
[2] *Gram.* I, 202, § 217.   [3] *Boeve*, p. lviii.

circumstances which influenced each individual scribe. The texts cited by Sturzinger and Stimming[1] for *e* are comparatively late, Adgar, Angier, *Auban*, etc. (*em, fleves, selt, velt,* etc.). I note *hem* (and in tonic position) in *Arundel Psalt.*[2]

6. ORTHOGRAPHIC VARIANTS.

a. *oe.* This is found with great frequency in Norman and Anglo-Norman texts, particularly at the beginning of words, and is supposably a device of the scribes to distinguish *ue* (= *ue* < Q) from *ue* (= *ve*), by designating the former as *oe.*[3] Cf. p. 70.

b. *oi (ui).* *oi* is an orthography which occurs quite frequently. Stimming[4] gives examples from *Brandan, Tristan,* Chardri, *Boeve,* and a few other texts, as *estoit (estuet), voit* (VŎLET), *poit (puet),* etc. (He omits the one from *Cumpoz* L, cited by Suchier,[5] *bois* < BŎVES.) Stimming suggests that we have here a case of "umgekehrte Schreibung" (as in *ie = e <* A cf. p. 39); he starts from the forms *estet, vet, pet,* etc. These the scribe ignorantly restores (?) to *estoit, voit, poit,* because he confuses them with derivatives of original *ę* (< Ē, Ĭ), for which *oi* was the proper continental equivalent (and by no means foreign to Anglo-Norman; cf. p. 50). This explanation does not appeal to me, though I do not insist on my own way of considering the variant in question. It seems to me that if the scribes had confused the *e* of *ue* with the *e* of *ei* < E, we might look for some other variant of the letter *e,* and certainly for *ei* rather than *oi,* which is not a regular Anglo-Norman product (cf. p. 50). No *ei (ai)* is recorded, so far as I am aware, as a variant of the *e* for *ue,* though it occurs for every other Anglo-Norman *e* (as for *e <* A, p. 40, and for *ę,* p. 57). Furthermore, the *e* for *ue* seems to have been comparatively late (cf. p. 73) and not particularly frequent. I prefer to use as starting-points toward *poit, estoit,* the forms *pot, estot,* which are present in

---

[1] *Boeve,* p. 208.   [2] *Zt* XII, 23, 24.
[3] Cf. Meyer-Lubke, *Gram* I, 196, 198, § 211 ; *Litblt.* I, 223.
[4] *Boeve,* p. 208.   [5] *Gram.* p. 41.

Anglo-Norman from the beginning (cf. p. 70). These (*pot*, *estot*) the scribe changed to *poit, estoit*, just as he corrected (?) other simple vowels by adding *ı* (*a* > *ai*, *e* > *ei*, *u* > *uı*, cf. pp. 50, 53, and 68) on account of the frequency with which his eye encountered *ai, ei, uı* which had developed from *a, e, u* (*o, ǫ*) before palatals. To my mind *oi* for *ǫ* corresponds to *ui* for *o* (*u*). For *oi* < *ǫ* + palatal, cf. p. 80, § 30.

The *uı* which Stimming cites for only one text (*Ipomedon*) doubtless reflects the scribe's pronunciation of the *oi* (i.e. *oi*) which is often used by him for *ǫ*.

   c. *eo*. We have already noted (p 53) the use of *eo* for checked *ẹ*. We find *eo* likewise for *ue* (or rather for a development of *ǫ*) before oral and nasal consonants (cf. below, § 29), and as so used it constitutes another peculiarity of Anglo-Norman manuscripts: *Oxf. Psalt., Camb. Psalt. veolt, eovre ; Arund. Psalt. veolt,*[1] Roland *deol*, etc.[2] It may seem illogical not to treat *eo* = *ẹ* and *eo* = *ǫ* together; we can easily conceive of the pronunciation *é-o* for the *eo* < *ẹ* (*fe-orm*) because the *o* can be considered as a glide sound, we might think of *eo* in *deol* or *veolt* or *heom* as being similarly pronounced, the *o* being a glide from the *e* to *l* or *m*; but, as I have indicated on previous pages, examples from our texts do not show that *e* for *ue* was early enough or frequent enough to allow us to take it as a basis for explaining early variants (like the present *eo*, or like the *oi* treated in the previous section) of the developments of *ǫ* In order to discover the value of the sound indicated by *eo* (for *ue*), one safe method is to observe other signs used for *ue* in the texts in which *oe* occurs, especially other signs of known value. Those of (supposedly) known value are *e* and *o*, the latter usually being taken to indicate a sound like modern French *eu*; such a value for *eo* (i.e. *eu*) was suggested very early.[3]

---

[1] *Zt* XII, 24.

[2] For texts and examples, cf. Stimming, *Boeve*, pp. 207, 208 ; Such. *Gram.* p 41 ; *Zt.* I, 569 ; Sturzinger, *Orth. Gall* pp. 44–46.

[3] Koschwitz, *Ueberlieferung*, p. 29.

Again, there is no question but that *eo* was used as the equivalent of a known *ę* (cf. p. 53) at one time (though not in earliest Anglo-Norman), just as *ea* was used for *ę*.[1] Consequently we might say that at one time (comparatively early) *eo* was equivalent to *eu*, at another (later) to *ę*. There can be no doubt about the latter use of *eo* (for *ę*), but I question the conclusiveness of the opinions that assign a value *é-o*, or *eu*, to *eo* for the earlier stages of the Anglo-Norman. I would suggest the following : The regular representatives of *ǫ* in Anglo-Norman were *o*, *eu*, *u*, and *e*. The appearances of *o*, *ö*, *ø*, and *eo* coincide; *ö*, *o*, and *eo* were devices of the scribes to indicate a sound of *o* that was not the simple *ǫ*, nor yet the distinct diphthong *ue*, but an approach to a diphthong which the scribe did not know exactly how to designate. Between *ǫ* and *ue* there existed another development for *ǫ*, just as between *ę* and *ie* there was an indefinite *ee* (cf. p. 41). This indefinite sound for *ǫ* was the one our scribes were trying to fix, and the various signs used (*ö*, *o*, and *eo*) reflect their uncertainty. It seems to me that *oe* too might well have originated in the same way; that is, as a graphic sign for the indefinite sound referred to. Later, it found a fixed place in orthography because it lent itself to indicating a necessary distinction between *ue* and *ve* (cf. p. 74).

d. *ou*. Stimming gives an example of *ou* from *Boeve*, -*sour* (SOROR), *soure*, and refers to *bouf* (BOVEM) in *William of Palermo*.

e. *ø*. This sign occurs in *Camb. Psalt.*, *iløc*, *pøple*, etc.[3] Suchier speaks of it as indicating the sound *ö* (*eu*).[4] Cf. my remarks above (c).

f. *ö*. Examples for this have been cited[5] for the *Oxf. Psalt.* only : *pöple*, *repröce*, *öïl*, and *ölie*. Compare my remarks above (c).

---

[1] Such. *Gram.* p. 42.   [2] *Boeve*, p. 208.   [3] Such. *Gram.* p. 41.
[4] Cf. Vising, *Jhrsbrcht.* II, 1, 250.
[5] Such. *Gram.* p. 41.

25. CHECKED Q.

Here we make note of two points: the presence of *ou* for the ǫ, and the rhyming of ę̄ : ǫ.

1. OU. It goes without saying that checked ǫ remains in most cases. Stimming[1] finds only one example of *ou*: *toust* from *Boeve* and Bozon. I add *cours* (CORDIBUS) from *Arund. Psalt.*[2] Stimming thinks that the word *oustent* (OBSTANT, *Boeve*) may point to an *u* (ǫ) as a phonetic variant of checked ǫ in Anglo-Norman. This point demands further study.

2. ǫ.o. Aside from the cases in which the ǫ occurs before a nasal (cf. p. 78, § 23), there is little evidence in favor of such a rhyme. Mall had supposed that such might be the case for the *Cumpoz* and *Bestiaire*, but Walberg[3] affirms that the ǫ rhymes only with itself in the *Bestiaire* and corrects Mall's examples.

26. LŎCUM, FŎCUM, JŎCUM.

I do not attempt to say anything new about the various forms of these words, but shall simply refer to places where the Anglo-Norman variants (*lieu, liu, leu*, etc.; *gieu, giu, ju, geu*, etc; *feu, fu, fou*, etc.) are especially mentioned or discussed.[4]

I shall, however, call attention to the form *lui* (*luis*). No mention is made of it in the bibliography cited, except by Stimming, who finds one example of *milui* in *Boeve* and supposes it may be another case of "umgekehrte Schreibung" (*lu* > *lui*, confusion with etymological *ui*, cf. p. 68). The cases of its occurrence, however, seem sufficiently numerous to justify our giving *lui* a place beside the other variants of LOCUM in Anglo-Norman; perhaps it is worthy

---

[1] *Boeve*, p. 189.   [2] *Zt.* XI, 515   [3] *Ibid.* XI, xlv.
[4] The best short statement for them in Anglo-Norman (and Norman) is that of Such. *Gram.* pp 53 and 56. Cf. in this connection Meyer-Lubke, *Gram.* I, 190, § 196; Uhlemann, *Auban*, p. 572 (here we find additional bibliography); Stimming, *Boeve*, p 204, Walberg, *Bestiaire*, p. xlvii; Busch, *Laut- und Formenlehre*, p. 35.

of further study, too. I note the following: *Arundel Psalt.*
lui[1] (in connection with *lui* the form *lai*[2] < LACUM is to be
observed); *Brandan*, l. 86; Denis Pyramus, *Vie St. Edmond*,
l. 729, *lui* (not in rhyme); *Madeleine*, 7, d, *luis*, and 10, c,
luis: pluis; Apocalypse: milui, 218 (p. 208), *lui : celui*, 340,
247 (p. 209), *luis : tuiz*, 310 (p. 211), *lui:fui* (past. particip.
of *fuir*), 948; one example of *fu* (preterite of *être*) : *fui*
(FOCUM), 843 (p. 232).

27. Q BEFORE A PALATAL.

We shall treat the *ui* arising from this combination in
connection with the similar *ui* < *ū* before a palatal, p. 80,
§ 33. There, too, will be considered the variant *oi*.

28. Q BEFORE L MOUILLÉE.

Here Anglo-Norman offers nothing new. I note the form
orguoil in the *Arundel Psalt.*[3] (cf. *orguel*[4]); in Angier (l. 32)
we find the reduction of *ue* to *e* in *veil = vueil*.

29. Q BEFORE A NASAL.

I considered ǫ before a nasal in connection with ǫ before
a nasal in those cases in which ǫ did not diphthongize (cf.
p. 69). It does not diphthongize when checked, of course,
and even in free position *o* alternates in about equal proportion with *ue*. The use of these two in our earlier texts
is given by Suchier.[5] We find *u* (*hume*) and *e* (*hem*), too,
just as before oral consonants.[6]

Examples of the usual variants for ǫ before consonants
occur here also. We note *oe* in *Arundel Psalt.*: *boens, soens;*[7]
eo is found, as in *Camb. Psalt.* and *Q. L. R.*: *heom, seon;*
the *Q. L. R.* shows *ueo* also: *hueom.*[8] Stimming finds one
or two examples of *ou* (*moun*) and *ui* (*suyn*) in *Boeve.*

[1] *Zt.* XII, 11.   [2] *Ibid.* XII, 14.   [3] *Ibid.* XI, 520.   [4] *Ibid.* XII, 19.
[5] *Gram.* pp. 73, 74. Add *Lois Gme.* p. xlvii.
[6] Cf. *Oxf. Psalt.* (Harseim, p. 203), *Camb. Psalt.* (Schumann, p 36),
Q. L. R. (Schlosser, p. 43), Angier, *Auban, Boeve;* Stimming, p. 209.
[7] *Zt.* XII, 23, 39.   [8] Such. *Gram.* p. 74; *Zt.* I, 569.

30. Ǫ BEFORE N MOUILLÉE.

Suchier[1] treats this point. There are, apparently, only two words of importance to be discussed, COGNITUM and LONGE + s. In *queinte*, the *uei* is kept (*u* going with the *q*); I note an additional example of *queinte* in Pyramus, *St. Edmond*, l. 934; *lueinz* does not occur but may be supposed from *luein* (*Camb. Psalt.* IX, 21).

31. PRETONIC O.

We have already noted (p. 66, § 21) the tendency of some of our earlier texts to keep *o* pretonic, and have seen that they may even substitute this *o* for an original *u* < *ū*. For pretonic *o* we find the usual variants, *u* and *ou*, before both oral and nasal consonants: cf. in the *Arundel Psalt.* for example, *oureilles, bounourez*.[2] The variants *i* and *e* are likewise to be noted (*connisez, apresmer*).[3] For the fall of the pretonic *o* in hiatus in verb forms (*oust*, etc.), cf. p. 60, § 17, 1, a (These remarks apply equally to *ę* and *ǫ*, since *ę* becomes *ǫ* in pretonic position.)

U

32. 1. U : O AND U : I. There are two points to be noted here, the rhyming of *ü : u* (*ǫ*) and that of *ü . i*. We have already considered the former (p. 66) and referred to the phonetic value of the *u* < *ū*. Obviously we cannot claim a pure *ü* for the entire period of Anglo-Norman, or in any case for the entire territory which that dialect represents.

The rhyming of *ü : i* deserves attention, more on account of its apparent peculiarity than its frequency. The references for it are given by Stimming.[4] Already in the *Cumpoz* we have *lune : embolisme*. We may add an example from *Vie Gregoire*, line 439: *truisses : peusses*. Vising[5] says

---

[1] *Gram.* p. 75. [2] *Zt* XI, 528, XII, 20.
[3] Examples and texts are given by Stimming, *Boeve*, p. 205.
[4] *Boeve*, p. lvi. *Étude*, p. 73.

that the *i* indicates nothing with regard to the pronunciation of the *u* ($< \bar{u}$) in Anglo-Norman.   The scribes, not
accustomed to hearing the French *ü*, confounded it with *i*;
moreover, it seems that the examples here are in part taken
from verb endings, where *-is, -it, -irent,* and the like could
easily replace *-us, -ut, -urent,* etc., by analogy.

2. ORTHOGRAPHIC VARIANTS (UI, O).   The *ui* for *ü* has
already been referred to (p. 68).[1]   (For the opposite, i.e. *ü*
instead of etymological *ui*, see below, § 33.)   Where there
is a confusion of *u* ($\bar{u}$) and *u* (o) we are not surprised to find
o substituted at times for etymological *u* ($< \bar{u}$), though examples are, apparently, not numerous:[2] *josque, couve,* etc.
(cf. above, p. 66, § 21).   We find the *o* before a nasal, too,
as *chescone.*

33. U (AND Q) BEFORE A PALATAL.

The phenomena encountered for the *ui* $<$ ǫ + palatal and
$< \bar{u}$ + palatal are, naturally, the same.

1. UI, U, AND I.   The pronunciation of *üi* wavered, in
Anglo-Norman, between *üi* and *ui*; the original accentuation was, doubtless, *üi*; this is shown, in part, by the early
and the persistent use of *u* for *ui*; *i* for *ui* was less frequent,
though it is early.   Details of the history of these two variants merit further study; in character, for example, *üi*
rhymes with final *ü*, and *üir* with *ü* + *r*, but *üit* not with
ü + *t*; this seems to indicate that before *t* the pronunciation may have been *ui*, and, consequently, *üt* and *uit* would
have made no rhyme.

The *ü* ($< üi$) may rhyme with *u* (ǫ) just like original *ü*,
as in Gaimar, *tuz : destruit.*[3]

2. OI.   We find *oi* in our texts substituted for the
ui $< \bar{u}$ + palatal and for the *ui* $<$ ǫ + palatal; as used

---

[1] Cf. Stimming, *Boeve,* p. 193.

[2] Cf. Stimming, *Boeve,* p. 193 ; Such. *Gram.* p. 64.

[3] For § 33, 1, cf. Meyer-Lubke, *Gram.* I, 82, § 62 ; *Litblt.* II, 359;
Stimming, *Boeve,* p. 209 ; Such. *Gram.* p. 35.

for the former, it furnishes another example of Anglo-Norman confusion of orthographies (cf. above, p. 74, where *ui* is substituted for the irregular *oi* representing free ǫ). Already in the *Cumpoz* (L) we note *loist, join*.[1] As used for *ui* < ǫ + palatal, the *oi* may be a reminiscence of the original ǫj before diphthongization (> *uei, ui*), just as we have original *o* in free position reflected in the *o* of our early texts (cf above, p. 70, § 24, 1); in some monuments *oi* occurs for *ui* < ǫj, but not for *ui* < ūj, and these same texts do not confuse *u* (ǫ) and *u* (ū); this, of course, points to a historical *oi* (for ǫj); later texts, however, doubtless use *oi* or *ui* indiscriminately.[2]

3. UE. This orthography (for *ui*) is particularly noteworthy in Angier; some examples are *pues, puessent, nuet, mues* (MODIOS;[3] this *ue* can be reduced to *u puSse, pussent*. The word PRŎXIMUM numbers *pruesme* and *prusme Oxf. Psalt., Q L. R*) among its derivatives; these and other variants of the same word occur in general French, however, and the *ue* of *pruesme* may not represent the same phenomenon as that recorded for Angier.[4]

CONSONANTS

The only general tendency, if we may call it such, to be noted in connection with Anglo-Norman consonants, is the fondness of the scribes for double consonants; the doubling is not confined to consonants of any one class, liquids, dentals, palatals, or labials, but all are treated alike and subjected to the process, regardless of etymological justification. Stimming gives examples and texts;[5] many instances are to be found in Angier:[6] *soccors, achettée, obbedience, relligion,*

---

[1] Mall, p. 64; Such. *Gram.* p. 35.

[2] Cf. Such. *Gram.* p. 59; Vising, *Étude*, p. 86; Paris, *Vie St. Gilles*, p. xxxi.   [3] Cf. Meyer, *Rom.* XII, 196; Cloran, *Dialogues*, p. 50.

[4] Cf. Such. *Gram.* p. 60.   [5] *Boeve*, p. 240.

[6] Meyer, p. 198; Cloran, p. 52.

G

reddevance, douzze, etc. I note in *Arundel Psalt., pleinne, orreilles, tuitte;* [1] in *Brandan, frerre,* l. 85; in *Sardenai,* 239, *chappele;* in *Apocalypse,* 111, *dittez. Vitte* has an explanation of its own (cf. below, p. 93, § 39). These double consonants have usually been considered to possess no especial phonetic significance, but recent investigations go to show that they may reflect an actual pronunciation of French consonants by the English.[2]

M AND N

34. We treat these two together because about the only thing noteworthy in connection with them is their interchange, and this is not at all peculiar to Anglo-Norman, though very frequent there; such frequency has always attracted the attention of editors, and they have studied the phenomenon from the point of view of the kind of consonant following the *m* or the *n*; the kind of vowel preceding the *m* or *n*; the bearing of the history of the *m, n* on the question of the nasalization of the vowels in Anglo-Norman, etc. Consequently some notice is here necessary.

1. INTERCHANGE. In Anglo-Norman we must not expect the regular French rule of *m* + dental > *n*; *n* + labial > *m* to be carried out consistently; there exists no apparent regularity. *n*, for example, occurs before labials in many texts, from the very earliest, in *Lois Guillaume,* XLVIII, we have *menbres,* in *Oxf. Psalt., enblancet,* etc.[3] Before *f,* Anglo-Norman has a fondness for *m*:[4] *emfant, gumfanun,* etc.

2. N AFTER R. The history of *n* in words like *jurn,*

---

[1] *Zt.* XI, 526, 516 ; XII, 46.

[2] I refer here to the researches of Morsbach, published in *Beiträge zur Roman. und Eng. Philologie.* Festgabe fur W. Foerster. Halle, 1902, pp. 324–330. Cf. *Rom.* XXXI, 618; cf. below, p. 89, *rr,* and p. 99, *cc.* From the last reference we shall see that the suggestion of a phonetic value for the double consonants was not new in the case of *cc,* at least.

[3] Examples, Stimming, *Boeve,* p. 215.   [4] *Ibid.* p. 216.

emfern, has attracted the especial attention of editors. It
is, naturally, of most importance in poetical texts. In the
earliest of these, the *Cumpoz*, it already shows signs of disappearance (*enfer*:*fer*), though by the side of such rhymes,
examples occur proving the pronunciation of the *n*, and it
seems to have preserved its value sometimes even in combinations like *enferns*, *corns*. Editors of texts subsequent to
the *Cumpoz*, however, agree that this *n* is silent in their
texts, having no phonetic value, even when written (as is
often the case).[1]

3. M AND N FINAL. A distinction between these two
is observed only in the *Lois Guillaume* and the *Oxf. Psalt*,
among our texts [2]

4. M AND N AND THE NASALIZATION OF VOWELS. Some
reference to this important subject seems necessary; as in
general French, the difficulties are encountered in the early
stages of the language. We introduce a note on the question here because the interchange of *m* and *n* is supposed to
have a bearing upon the point, and because *m* and *n* have
been spoken of as having varying values after different
vowels.

For example, Koschwitz,[3] in speaking of *mum pecchiet*,[4]
Oxf. Psalt. XXIV, 12, says the appearance of *m* for *n*
before a labial, which often occurs in Anglo-Norman (he
here cites examples), proves that in this dialect *m* (*n*) does
not form a nasal combination with the preceding vowel.

Again, Mall,[5] speaking for the *Cumpoz*, says. *m* and *n*
are kept distinct (forms like *emposet*, 730, are rare); the
only exception is in the rhyme *ums* : *uns*, *om*. *on*, and he explains this exception by saying that nasalization was very
old in (*ou*) + *m*(*n*).[6]

---

[1] Cf. for example, Walberg, *Best* p. lvi ; Paris, *Gme. de Berneville*,
p. xxxii ; Stimming, *Boeve*, pp. x and 216.

[2] Such. *Litblt*. XXII, 121.   [3] *Zt*. II, 488.

[4] *Mum* is one of Meister's corrections ; cf. Meister, pp. 108 and 118.

[5] p. 76.   [6] Cf. Walberg, *Best*. p. lvi.

These two statements, the one proving the status of the vowel from that of the consonant, the other that of the consonant from that of the vowel, mutually complete each other. The idea of Koschwitz seems to be that in a nasal combination the separate identity of *m* as a labial and of *n* as a dental would be lost: if *mun pecchiet* had been pronounced *mũn pecchiet*, the speaker or hearer would have been aware of no abrupt break from the *mũn* to the *pecchiet;* but *mum pecchiet* proves that the pronunciation was at first *mu-n pecchiet*, and, to avoid having a dental (*n*) followed directly by a labial (*p*) the *n* was changed to a labial (*m*). This change of *n* to *m* to suit a following consonant indicates that *m* and *n* had their distinct values, which they would not have had if the preceding *u* had formed a nasal combination with the *n*. This is further illustrated by Mall's example, where such a loss of individual values is illustrated by the rhyming of *um : un*, in which we have to suppose a nasal value for the *u*.

Thus the two statements fit into each other. The separate identity of the consonant in the first case proves nonnasalization; nasalization in the second case explains the non-individuality of the consonants. After all, however, the two writers meant to assert two things, Koschwitz, non-nasalization, Mall, interchangeableness of *m* and *n*. The first proves non-nasalization by interchangeableness; the second, interchangeableness, by nasalization.

This is about as far as a study of the question of nasalization in the writings of our editors will lead. A general presentation of the point is given by Suchier.[1] The convincing statement for the early history of the nasalization of the vowels, not only in Anglo-Norman, but in general French, is yet to be formulated. Maybe the solution is to be discovered in Anglo-Norman ; there is a great advantage in beginning the study with that dialect, because we know that nasalization disappeared there toward the end of the

[1] *Gram.* p. 61.

thirteenth century,[1] only a century and a half after the date
of our first texts; the circumstances of the disappearance of
nasalization so soon after its appearance ought to throw
some light on the manner of that appearance; principles
thus obtained might apply to general French.

5. Miscellaneous.

Stimming[2] considers the following points: —

a. Confusion of *n* and *l* (*alne*) We may add a similar
confusion of *n* and *r*; for example, in *Vie Gregoire* occurs
joevres (= *jeunes*) lines 958, 1552, and in *Vie St. Thomas*
III, 87, 88 we note a similar *jo(u)vre*.

b. Confusion in orthography of *n* and *gn: digner = diner.*
We note an example of this in *Sardenai,*[3] *moigne* (the regular
moine is the rule, however).

c. Loss of etymological *n: covendra.*

d. Insertion of an inorganic *n: ensi, boins.* In *Arundel
Psalt.* we note *seigne* (= *seige* for *siege*).[4]

I consider below the Anglo-Norman form *verms* (p. 114,
§ 54), and the peculiar ending -*ánie*, < N + J (p. 90, § 37, 3).

L

35. L (BEFORE A CONSONANT).

I have little to note here that is remarkable. There is no
well-defined usage confined to any particular period. If we
should endeavor to divide the examples from our texts under
the headings '*l* remains,' '*l* falls,' '*l* > *u*' we would find one
and the same text often illustrating all three. Neither will
a division of the examples according to the vowel preceding
the *l* justify itself. The state of affairs in the older texts is
the following: previous to *Brandan, l* is kept quite consistently: *Cumpoz, l* remains;[5] *Bestiaire, l* remains as a rule,
falls in the group -*els;*[6] in *Lois Guillaume,* where one Ms.

---

[1] Cf. Stimming, *Boeve,* p. 218. [2] *Boeve,* pp. 216–218.
[3] *Rom* XIV, 88. [4] *Zt.* XII, 46.
[5] Mall, pp. 65, 77. [6] Walberg, pp. liii, liv.

shows $l > u$, the variants from all the other Mss. will show the l to be kept. There is only one word in the whole text with $l > u$ for which no variant showing the l kept is given;[1] *Oxf. Psalt.*, l remains, but a weakening is evident because of the presence of a glide e, *chalemeals*. Before flexional s, l is sometimes lost, though examples showing this are in a minority;[2] *Camb. Psalt*, l remains; in rare cases it falls or $> u$;[3] *Q. L. R.*, l remains. Schlosser studied in detail[4] the history of the l after various vowels. The exceptions are *autre, autel*, and *fiz*; *Oxf. Roland*, l is kept; glide e appears exceptionally.

With the *Brandan* the weakening of the l becomes the rule;[5] by the side of *beals, oiseals*, that text shows *beus, oiseus*. Gaimar knew the vocalization.[6] In Angier the l can remain, fall, or become u.[7] Chardri and Gme. de Berneville both illustrate the vocalization $> u$.[8]

1. L > U.

The earliest known examples of $l > u$ in Anglo-Norman occur in the *Domesday Book* (date, 1086) in the proper names *Bauduin, Tetbaut*.[9] There is little doubt but that l had the value of u in many cases when retained in orthography, and editors of early poems are sometimes constrained to say that while they do not find rhymes attesting the vocalization of l, neither do they find rhymes proving that the vocalization might not have taken place.[10] It is evident that vocalization of $l > u$ was known very early in Anglo-Norman; it became common toward the end of the thirteenth century.

---

[1] Such. *Litblt.* XXII, 121.   [2] Harseim, p. 320.

[3] Schumann, p. 43.   [4] pp. 6, 21, 28, 38, 39, 48, 53.

[5] Forster, *Zt.* I, 565.   [6] Vising, *Étude*, p. 87.   [7] Cloran, p. 52.

[8] Koch, pp. xxx, xxxiii, xxxvii ; Paris, p. xxiv.

[9] *Zt.* VIII, 361, § 39 ; for the earliest examples in French proper cf. *Rom.* XVII, 428.

[10] Cf. for example, Vising, *Étude*, p. 77 (*Brandan*); Walberg, *Best.* p. liii.

2. L Lost.

The simple loss of the *l* is likewise attested by frequent examples from the time of the earliest texts;[1] the two phenomena, *l* > *u* and *l* lost, seem to have been present side by side, with little or no time difference in the process of their change. We have an indication in the *Orthographia Gallica* that *l* became *u* when *l* was preceded by *a*, *e*, or *o*; this coincides with the fact that the earliest examples in rhyme for the loss of *l* are when the *l* was preceded by *i* or *u*. The rule of the *Orthographia Gallica* doubtless represents the original state of affairs[2]

3. Final L > U (or Lost).

Final *l* preceding a word beginning with a consonant may become *u*. This is an extension of the vocalization of the *l* in the body of a word, appears later, and is at first confined to proclitic words like *del* and *al*; it is frequently found in *teu*, *queu* (*tel*, *quel*) too. Sturzinger gives references.[3] We may add *Vie St. Thomas*, *teu pes* (I, 56), *ceu jour* (III, 40). This *teu* is used with feminines both in Chardri and *Vie St. Thomas* (*teu joie*, IV, 85). We note also *nu* = *ne le*, *Bible Fragment*, 854; *eu* = *en l*, *Apocalypse*, 378, 623. In the *Apocalypse* we find the *u* before a vowel too, *solau oscures*, *solau e*, 413, 430.

The same analogy (to *l* + consonant in the interior of words) will explain the occasional loss of final *l*, particularly in unaccented words, *a*, *de*, *ne*, and the like (for *al*, *del*, *nel*).[4]

4. Miscellaneous.

a. Confusion of *l* and *r*. The confusion is frequent from the time of the earliest texts. Cf. *Bestiaire, nature : nule*, Gaimer, *Contraire : bataille*, *Vie St. Gilles, apostorie : historie; Apocalypse, itel : mer* (line 1228).[5]

---

[1] Reference in Stimming, *Boeve*, p. 211.

[2] See the full note and references of Sturzinger, *Orth Gall.* p. 50, VII, T. 11.

[3] *Orth. Gall.* p. 50.   [4] Cf. Stimming, *Boeve*, p 212.

[5] Cf. Walberg, *Best.* p. lv; Stimming, *Boeve*, p. 212.

b. $l + j > r$. This development is noted by Paris[1] not only for original l as in *apostolie; apostorie;* cited above, but even for the $l < d$, as seen in the proper name *Gidie, Gilie, Gile, Gire.*

c. Inorganic *l.* There are a few examples of such an *l* both before consonants and final, as *voils = voix.*[2] In *Arundel Psalt.* I note *felulnie, elnemis.*[3]

36. L AND N MOUILLÉES.

1. LOSS OF PALATALIZATION. We have to note the loss of the palatalization of the *l* and *n* in Anglo-Norman. The fact that the palatalization can disappear not only when *l'* and *n'* precede consonants, but when they are intervocalic or final, and that the *l* from *l'* can become *u* just like original *l* before a consonant — these facts point to an early date for the loss. It became general in the course of the thirteenth century; we must not suppose, however, that the palatalized sounds were forgotten by our writers, for such was not the case.[4]

2. ORTHOGRAPHIC VARIANTS. It is interesting to note the numbers of variants for *l'* and *n'* that appear in the *Domesday Book.*[5] For *l'* we find *ilgi, ilg, illg, il, ill, illi, lg, llg, lli, ll;* for *n', ingi, ing, inc, ini, ign, in, inn, gn, ngi, ng, ni, nn.* This list might, apparently, embrace all varieties, but it does not include the *ignn* of the *Q. L. R.,* nor the *illl* of the same (the latter is an evident mistake, however),[6] nor the *igni* and *nni* of the *Camb. Psalt.*[7] Doubtless, a complete list for Anglo-Norman would offer additions to the

---

[1] *Gme. de Berneville,* p. xxxii.

[2] Cf. Stimming, *Boeve,* pp. 211, 212. [3] *Zt.* XI, 524, 525.

[4] The best general statement and references on the point are those of Vising, *Étude,* pp. 77, 78, and 87. He here speaks of the confusion of palatal and dental sounds in Gaimar and *Brandan* (cf. for the latter, *Zt.* IX, 100). For the *Cumpoz* and *Bestiaire,* cf. Walberg, p. liv (no examples of *n' : n* however, p. lvi); *Gme. de Berneville,* Paris, p. xxxii; *Boeve,* Stimming, pp. 212 and 218.

[5] *Zt.* VIII, 361, 362. [6] Schlosser, pp. 54, 61. [7] Schumann, p. 45.

above. Nevertheless, the favorite orthography for *l'* and *n'* in our texts seems always to have been simply *l* and *n*, or *il* and *in*.

R

37. Several interesting phenomena present themselves in connection with a study of this consonant.

1. R AND RR. The confusion of single and double *r* is noteworthy. Faulde pays especial attention to it in his article on gemination.[1] The grammarian Beza warned people against the carelessness of the Norman writers in this regard, and the carelessness is strongly reflected on English territory. Faulde indicates that the earliest instances of the simplification of *rr* occur when *rr* was preceded and followed by *e*. He cites cases from *Bestiaire*, *Oxf. Psalt*, and *Oxf. Roland*. Meyer-Lubke[2] speaks of *tr > rr* after the accent as especially Anglo-Norman, though he adds at once that *r* is found too, and already in the *Cumpoz* ("*piere arriere*," l. 2745[3]); Stimming[4] gives examples and text references; Andresen gives instances from *Amadas et Ydoine*, and refers to others in the Anglo-Norman Mss. of the *Reimpredigt*, and of the *Lois* of Marie de France.[5] Walberg,[6] for the *Bestiaire*, decides to adopt *r* in all cases except foreign words and the future of *seeir* (to avoid confusion with the same tense of *estre*). We have already referred to the *Arundel Psalt.*, *orreilles* (p. 82).

It seems fruitless to endeavor to make any definite statement for the *r* and *rr*. To divide our examples according to the place of the accent, or according to the etymological background of the *r* (as *r*, *rr*, *tr*, etc), or study the futures (in which so many cases are met), — all leads to but one conclusion: we are in the presence of another instance of mere confusion.

---

[1] *Zt.* IV, 547   [2] *Gram* I, 446, § 495, 490, § 548
[3] This is an incorrect citation, the rhyme is *pieres : manieres*.
[4] *Boeve*, p. 214.   [5] *Zt.* XIII, 86.   [6] p. lxxxix.

2. R BEFORE A CONSONANT. The loss of the *r* when preceding a consonant is often to be noted in Anglo-Norman, and proves the weak pronunciation of the *r*: *reto(r)ner, se(r)fs,* etc. Stimming gives references and examples.[1] We cite, in addition, the following: in *Sardenai,* 447, occurs the rhyme *dame : arme* (where *arme* = ANIMA); in *Apocalypse,* is *oscurs : puz ;* in the same, 25, we find *nurves : pointures.* Anglo-Norman thus adds its quota to the many indications we have of an early, general weakening of *r* + consonant throughout Old French.[2]

3. R + I. Here we must call attention to the endings *-arie, -erie, -orie* (and similarly *-anie, -enie, -onie*). These occur in Anglo-Norman as *-árie, -érie, -ánie,* etc., as *-aire, -eire, -aine,* etc., and, finally, as *-aríe, -eríe, -aníe,* etc. The first set, *-árie,* etc., is represented in English words like *primary, victory ;* the second *-aire,* etc., is the regular French form; the third, *aríe,* etc., occurs in the latter stages of Anglo-Norman (*victorie : vie*), — Uhlemann specifies shortly before or after the date of *Auban.*[3]

4. R AFTER A CONSONANT.

a. *e* inserted (*fauderai,* etc.). This point has already been discussed (cf. p. 61, § 17, 2).

b. *r* lost. Editors have cited but few examples for this; the instances in Gaimar are well known : *estre : feste, ancestre : geste, entrent : dementent.*[4] In *Vie Gregoire* I note *Theotiste : epistre,* l. 1673. We have to do mostly with the group *-str* (cf. below, no. 6, where an inorganic *r* is inserted after *-st*).

5. METATHESIS OF R. This is of very frequent occurrence in Anglo-Norman, though by no means confined to that dialect.

---

[1] *Boeve,* pp. liii and 215.

[2] Cf. here the important remarks and references of Neumann, *Litblt.* VI, 241, f.-n. 2.

[3] Cf. on this point, Vising, *Étude,* pp. 71, 82 ; Mall, *Cumpoz,* p. 55 ; Uhlemann, *Auban,* p. 569 ; Walberg, *Best.* XLV, LXXXV ; Grass, *Adam,* 125 ; Meyer, *Rom.* XXV, 256.

[4] Cf. Vising, *Étude,* p. 87 ; Kupferschmidt, p. 418.

a. *-re > -er.* The most frequent examples of metathesis in our texts are met in connection with forms of the verb *prendre; pernons, pernez,* etc. ; such are found from the time of the very earliest prose and poetical texts; in addition to these, a few cases like *ester < estre, quater < quatre,* are cited.[1] I note, in addition, from *Mélanges, pover = povre;*[2] *Vie St. Edmond,* 882, *overs = ovres;* and from *Apocalypse, liver,* 296, 300, 304, etc., by the side of *livere;* also *quater,* 310, 329. It looks as if, in some of these cases, there may have been a development such as *livre > livere > liver.*

b. *-er > -re.* There may be a question whether certain verbs which apparently show a change of conjugation do not rather illustrate a metathesis of *r*; as *getter > gettre, lutter > luttre* (cf. Morphology, p 119)

6. INORGANIC R. Stimming[3] cites some examples from *Q. L. R.,* Gaimar, Bozon, and *Ipomedon.* In a number of cases the *r* follows *t* and *st* (*Olestre, destrin,* etc.), though *philosophre* is found. In *Aspremont,* I note *curorne,* 80, and entirely different from the above, *poreir = poeir* (*pouvoir*), 63.

7. INTERCHANGE OF L AND R. Here we have only to refer to page 87, where this point has already been treated.

P

38. We must note the Anglo-Norman development of P + J, which has been discussed as follows Mall[4] said that the sound of the *c < PJ* was *ts,* and quoted examples from Philippe de Thaun, *Q. L R,* Fantosme, etc. ; such was likewise the result of Varnhagen's extended study.[5] The decision of the question seems to have depended almost entirely upon the rhyming of the word *sace* (SAPIAT) with those words

*

[1] Stimming, *Boeve,* p. 213.   [2] *Rom.* IV, 376
[3] *Boeve,* p 215   [4] *Cumpoz,* p. 92
[5] *Zt.* III, 177 , cf. *Rom.* VIII, 625 (a summary of V.'s results).

in which a similar *c* had an assured value of *ts*, such as *tace*,
face, *glace*, etc.   Schlösser[1] has a long note on the point, including a review of the discussion: the *Q. L. R.* represents
the *c* < PJ by *c*, *ch*, *sch*, and *sc* (last two seldom); the *ch* and
sch, he says, indicate the pronunciation *č*[2] for *c* < PJ was not
unknown to the scribe of the *Q. L. R.*   If such is true of that
text and of the *Camb. Psalt. sace*,[3] it was doubtless true of
later texts; *č* is further indicated by English words like
approach ;[4] consequently we must suppose that Anglo-Norman knew both *ts* and *č* for the *c* < PJ, the older value being
ts.   Walberg[5] cites further examples of *c* having the value of
ts, saying that *sace : glace* is a Norman rhyme.

T, D

39. T AND D INTERVOCALIC.

Our texts show that Anglo-Norman, so swift in many of
its phonetic changes, preserves some of the rare examples ·
that represent the gradual disappearance of *t* and *d*, and
thus exemplifies the fact that the disappearance was very
much later in some portions of French dialect territory than
in others.[6]   The comparatively extensive use of the Anglo-
Saxon *th* in our texts makes it evident that the Normans
still pronounced the intervocalic dentals at the time of the
conquest, and that this pronunciation was continued in
Anglo-Norman for some time, till toward the middle of the
twelfth century in any case.[7]   That the pronunciation *th* or
dh was peculiar to Anglo-Norman is not sure.[8]
For our earliest texts we note the following :[9] In *Cumpoz*

---

[1] *Q. L. R.* p. 63.   [2] I use *č* as equivalent to *ch* in English *church*.
[3] Schumann, p. 50.   [4] Stimming, *Boeve*, p. 235.   [5] *Best.* p. lxvii.
[6] I here refer to Lot's researches, *Rom.* XXX, 481 *ss.*
[7] See here the statement and references of Kluge and Baist, *Zt.* XX,
330.   For useful references, cf. *Ibid.* p. 322.
[8] See note and reference by Paris, *Rom.* XVI, 156.
[9] Cf. Meyer-Lübke, *Gram.* I, 388, § 436.

and *Bestiaire* the dentals fall, with isolated exceptions.[1] In *Alexis* (L) *th* occurs very often. In *Lois Guillaume*, where the scribe omits the intervocalic dental constantly, we have one of the rare examples of the use of the Anglo-Saxon dental spirant sign, *đ* (*fieđe*).[2] In *Oxf. Psalt.* the dental is kept as a rule, though there are a number of examples of its fall. In past participles, forms with *d* are predominant; in other words the dental perseveres or is lost with no apparent regularity; or again, certain words, like *vie, crier, ocire*, never have the dental.[3] For the *Camb. Psalt.* Schumann[4] thinks that, in the original, the fall was well-nigh general; *th* occurs but once (*benetheit*, XXVII, 6). The *Q L R.* shows the same state of affairs as the *Cumpoz* and *Bestiaire*.[5]

We may deduce, from this evidence, that within a single dialect, here the Anglo-Norman, the fall of *t, d* took place more readily in some words than in others. This point is studied at length by Koschwitz[6] According to him the earliest cases of the fall are shown by Latin D + R (these two having been assimilated even in Latin times); then *d* (< T) + *r*; *d* + *ie*; *ai, ei*, etc. + *d*. A simple statement is given by Paris, too:[7] the *d* that disappears comes from *d* intervocalic, or *d* followed by *r* or *l* (*vidrent, Rodlant*), from *t* intervocalic (*vide, muder*) or followed by *r* or *l* (*podrons*) It must have been pronounced nearly like English *th* in *this*. It shows signs of disappearance at the epoch of the *Roland* and does fall shortly afterward.

The word *vite*, which is so persistent, even in texts showing in other cases the fall of the *t, d*,[8] and which is written *vitte* in the *Brandan* (l. 76), may be considered a learned word in this form (*vite*), used in referring to the recountal of the events in the life of a saint.[9]

---

[1] Mall, pp 79, 80 , Walberg, p lvii.
[2] Matzke, p. xlviii   [3] Harseim, p 321.
[4] p 47.   [5] Schlosser, p. 67.
[6] *Ueberlieferung*, pp. 58–60.   [7] *Extraits Roland*[4], p. 15.
[8] Cf. Walberg, *Best.* p. lvii.   [9] Paris, *Rom.* XXIX, 590, f.-n 1.

40. T AND D FINAL.

The state of affairs with regard to the final dentals is very confusing at first sight. For example: In the *Oxf. Psalt.* the *t* and *d* are kept quite regularly; in the original they were probably not always pronounced. We have lists of the verbs in this text showing the exact proportion of the fall or the maintenance of final dentals.[1] In the *Camb. Psalt.*, certain words always keep the final, others always drop it, others are irregular; there is a like inconsistency in verb forms, though in the last two parts of the *Psalter* a tendency to drop the finals is manifest; *t* > *d* seldom; we note seven instances of *th*;[2] I note *th* in *Arundel Psalt.*, *oth* (AUDIVIT).[3] In the *Q. L. R.* the dental remains as *d* (seldom *t*) or falls. Here, too, we have details for verbs and various words. After consonants *t* remains; there is one example of *th*.[4]

The pronunciation of these finals, where kept, depended on the elements following them. Both *t* and *d*, unsupported by other consonants, had two values previous to their disappearance, *th* (*thing*) and *th* (*this*), the former before pauses and voiceless explosives, for example; the latter before vowels, and before consonants other than the voiceless stops.

The manner and stages of disappearance of these finals have given rise to much discussion. Mall[5] supposed that final *t* was always pronounced in one manner — voiceless, and that it disappeared gradually, first after *e, i* (*Cumpoz*) next after *a* (*Bestiaire*), finally after *u*. Suchier[6] devotes some space to a refutal of Mall's position. He insists on the distinction between the fixed ("fest") and the shifting ("lose") dental (the *t* in *set* < SEPTEM is a "fest," the *d* in *feid* < FIDEM a "lose" dental). The two do not rhyme together regularly, and must have had different pronuncia-

---

1 Harseim, p. 322.
2 Schumann, pp. 47, 48.
3 *Zt.* XI, 515.
4 Schlosser, p. 68.
5 *Cumpoz*, p. 81 *ss.*
6 *Reimpredigt*, p. xix *ss.*

tions, the one ("fest") voiceless, the other ("lose") voiced. The final of *amed, venud* had the same value as the intervocalic *d* in *amede, venude* (except that the *d* of *amed* may have been pronounced as *d*, that of *amede* as *th*). When the *d* of *amede* began to fall in the course of the eleventh century, so did the *d* of *amed;* just as the writing of intervocalic *d* in the manuscripts was optional in the middle of the twelfth century, so was that of final *d* (but final *d* could interchange with *t*, intervocalic *d* could not).

The relative times of the loss of the finals Suchier thinks to have been the following. First of all, original etymological *d* fell. Perfects in *-it*, and *fit* (*fuit*) lost *t* as early as the eleventh century. Verbal forms in *-at* (perfects in *-at*, *at* < HABET, and futures constructed from infinitives + the present tense of HABERE), lost their *t* within literary times; that is, during and after the twelfth century. Suchier specifies the Norman and Anglo-Norman texts keeping, and those losing, the *t* after *a*.[1]

Vising[2] accepts Suchier's division of the two classes of dentals, and dwells upon the sharp line of demarcation between the fixed and the changeable dental. Walberg[3] goes over the whole question, formulating a scheme based on the statements of Suchier, and on those of Paris in the *Extraits Roland*. Walberg considers the examples under three headings. First: finals originally between two vowels, of which the second fell in French, and the final of atonic -AT. Here the *t* fell as early as the *Bestiaire, fei : lei*; examples are furnished likewise by the participial endings -ATUM, -ITUM. For the termination -AT, he makes a count of the rhyme *-e(t) : e*, of *e(t) : e(t)*, also of the elision of the *e* of *e(t)* Second: finals supported by other consonants; here the *t* remained steadfastly, *cuit : tuit*. Third: finals not supported by other consonants; here the final dental is lost; examples

---

[1] See here Stengel's remarks, *Litblt.* II, 329, Meyer-Lübke gives a summary of Suchier's results, *Gram.* I, 500, § 557.

[2] *Étude*, p. 89.   [3] *Bestiaire*, p. lvii *ss*.

are drawn from preterites in -*it*, -*at*, and *at* < HABET, also futures in -*at* < HABET. Walberg[1] questions two rhymes cited by Mall from the *Cumpoz* (preterites in -*it* rhyming with a fixed *t*); in this he is upheld by Paris.[2]

The above represents the merest outline of the question as it affects Anglo-Norman more especially. There are many interesting points of detail, even in our dialect, not spoken of here, but which are referred to in the citations given. Without a knowledge of these points the student will experience difficulty in assigning examples from any one text to places under the three divisions as given above. Because so many verb forms have final *t*, the investigator has to allow for analogies, crossings, and the like. Furthermore it must be borne in mind that even comparatively definite statements, like those of Suchier and Walberg, indicate only the general lines of development. In the study of some one poetical production, for example, it will have to be remembered that the finals, before completely disappearing, were pronounced or not pronounced according to the exigencies of the rhymes; and for each text the editor has to adopt some consistent scheme of orthography with regard to the dentals found in his text (as did Mall, Suchier, and Walberg,[3] among others).

41. T AND D MISCELLANEOUS.

1. CONFUSION OF T AND D IN GROUPS. Here we refer to Stimming;[4] we find, for example, *veindre*, *Bedleem*; *voutrions*, *pertriz*; *forment* illustrates the loss of the *t*.

2. FINAL T AND D.

a *t*, *d* < *z* (*ts*). This peculiar change was cited by Suchier,[5] early in our studies. It affects particularly the second person plurals in -*ez*. In *Camb. Psalt.* we note *seied*,

---

[1] *Bestiaire*, p. lxi, f.-n.   [2] *Rom.* XXIX, 590.
[3] Cf *Bestiaire*, p. xci.   [4] *Boeve*, pp. 221–223.
[5] *Auban*, p. 48. Cf. *Zt.* I, 570; *Litblt.* VI, 371; Stimming, *Boeve*, p. 230.

corned, and also an example from a past participle, *hied*
(*hez* = VINCTI), CI, 19. In this text the phenomenon is
noteworthy also because it affects the declension of the
nouns. *jugemend* for *jugemenz*, etc. Sometimes both *d* and
z are written, *mondz* = MONTES. The *d* may be assimilated
to a following consonant, *suz lever* > *sudlever* > *sullever*.
The same (*t* for *z*) occurs in *Brandan*, *seet*, *prenget* = *seez*,
prengez (cf. below, p 122, 5).

b. Final *t* > *d*. *d* for final *t* is a common orthographic
peculiarity of Anglo-Norman; *mound*, *mord*, etc.[1] The confusion of final *d* and *t* is very old, being found in the *Domesday Book*;[2] for that matter it goes back to Latin texts just
preceding the French period.[3]

c. Final *t* > *k* This change, found on the continent, appears in several instances in our dialect. Stimming[4] mentions examples from *Boeve: branc*, *renc*, etc., and refers to
others. For the same in first person singular present of
verbs, see below, p 120, § 62, **b** The *k* represents a mere
orthographic change in Anglo-Norman — a fact proved by
rhyme[5] To the examples mentioned we may add one from
Vie Gregoire, 2121, *Everwic : eslit.*

d. Final *t* lost. This is the most frequent of all the
phenomena mentioned, and applies to *t* in the interior
of the word as well as to final *t*. Examples occur from
the time of the earliest texts; *es* = *est*, *ai* = *ait*, *osa* = *osast*,
etc.[6]

e Inorganic final *t*. Such a *t* was added particularly
after *n*, and in this case, was pronounced: *tyrant*, *paysant*,
etc.[7] It is easy to see analogy here, and likewise in cases
where *t* is added after *s*, *mist* (MISSUM), *fist* (FECI); but after
other consonants, as *ert* (HERI), and after vowels, as *frait*
(= *ferai*) the *t* seems due only to indifferent orthography.

[1] *Boeve*, p. 221.   [2] *Zt* VIII, 360.
[3] Cf *Rom.* I, 327 ; *Zt* V, 45   [4] *Boeve*, pp. 221, 222
[5] Cf Sturzinger, *Orth Gall.* p. 52   [6] Stimming, *Boeve*, p. 222.
[7] Walberg, *Best.* p. lxiii.

H

C

42. The obscure points connected with the history of palatal *c* have little light thrown on them from a study of Anglo-Norman. This dialect not only offers nothing original or peculiar, but it reflects nearly every irregularity or peculiarity to be seen in French of the continent. As may be expected, all kinds of orthographies abound. " In one and the same manuscript we find the graphic signs of Central French and of South Norman by the side of those of Picard and North Norman, — a fact explained by the presence in England of immigrants from different provinces of France."[1] Koch[2] puts the case even more strongly when he says that in his opinion the sounds *k* and *ch* (not to speak of the signs used for them) were adopted inconsistently by one and the same individual. The three sounds, *k*, *ch*, and *ts* were all known to Anglo-Norman writers, and each was represented in several ways. Stimming[3] gives them as follows: —

1. C PRONOUNCED AS K. Here it was written *k* and *qu*, *q* being used only before *u*; *ch* too was used: *eschorcher*, *auchun*.

2. C PRONOUNCED AS TS. *c* is found here, not only before *e* and *i*, but before *a* and *o*; *co*, *comencat*, etc.; *sc* reflects the change from *ts* to *s* in pronunciation: *ascer* (for which change *s* alone is commonly written); many examples occur in *Sardenai;* for example, *sel*, 110, *sité* 21 [we find the opposite, *c* = *s*, in the same text, as *eucent*, 298, *auci*, 225, etc.]; *ss* occurs in *issi* (*ici*) several times. In both early and late texts *ch* occurs here too, and not infrequently; *feche* (*feis*), *pecha* (*pieca*), etc.

3. C PRONOUNCED AS CH. Here *c* is found quite often in the earlier texts, especially when preceding an *a* (*Domesday Book, Brandan, Oxf. Roland*). However, *ch* early became the popular way of denoting the sound *tsh* (*Brandan*,

---

[1] Meyer-Lubke, *Gram.* I, 357, § 410. [2] Chardri, p. xxxv.
[3] *Boeve*, pp. 231-236.

Cumpoz, Camb. Psalt., Q.L.R.). We find *cch*, too. Faulde,[1] noting the consistent retention of *cc* in *peccher* and *seccher* in texts of the twelfth century, in instances where continental texts show one *c*, says the pronunciation must have been *k-tsh*.

The presentation of the question by Stimming is as detailed as a work of the nature of the present one calls for. The palatals in each separate Anglo-Norman text furnish abundant subjects for investigation. For such investigations the students may look for models in works like those referred to in the foot-note below.[2]

G

43. The history of palatal *g* in Anglo-Norman is essentially the same as that of *g* in Central French. We have to note several varying orthographies. For example, *g* for *dž*, *goie, mangue, gambe; ch* for *dž, bercher, chambe.* To the examples given by Stimming[3] and Walberg[4] we may add some from *Arundel Psalt.*, where we find *ch* for *dž* in *vencheur, venchance,*[5] *g* for *dž* in *goie,*[6] and a combination of *g* and *ch* in *estreingchanz.* As may be expected, we find *j* for *g*; as *Camb. Psalt.* XXXVI, 21, *jable = gable*, and, in the same text, *g* before *e* with the same value as before *a*, as *orgeillus*, XXV, 4.

V

44 There is little that is characteristic to note with regard to *v*.

1. LOSS OF V IN GROUPS AND INTERVOCALIC. We have already referred (p. 91, § 37, 4, a) to the insertion of an *e* in

---

[1] *Zt* IV, 553. I note an example of *j* for *ch* in *Vie Gregoire*, 1598, *jasquns.*

[2] Varnhagen, *Das c im Orforder Psalter; Zt* III, 161–177 (cf *Rom.* VIII, 625) ; Buhle, *Das c im Lambspringer Alexius, Oxforder Roland und Londoner Brandan;* Greifswald, 1881 (cf *Litblt.* II, 441).

[3] *Boeve*, p. 237.   [4] *Bestiaire*, p xcii.

[5] *Zt.* XI, 519, 534.   [6] *Ibid.* XII, 4, 26, 52.

the group *vr*. The *v* of the combination is sometimes lost, as is shown in English words like *poor, kerchief,* and the like; several examples occur in *Boeve*.[1] We have a few instances, also, of the fall of the *v* intervocalic, though most of them occur in different forms of the verb *espoenter*.[2]

2. CONFUSION OF V AND F. This is common in Anglo-Norman and resembles the confusion of *t* and *d* (cf. p. 97). Cases occur as early as Gaimar (*nafrer, jofne*).[3] I notice in *Aspremont*, 43, *life* (= *lève*), *Apocalypse*, 144, 512, *escriferai*, 452, *chefuz* (both *v* and *f* are seen in *servfs*, 2).

W

45. *W* was a letter much favored in Anglo-Norman orthography, from the date of the earliest texts. In the *Camb. Psalt.* it is used in six different ways, as shown by the words *awrnement, eswarderai, ewes, ow (ou), towe (tue), swatume.*[4] Similar uses in other texts are referred to by Stimming.[5] It will be seen that in nearly all the *w* takes the place of the half-consonantal *u*. This usage is considered as peculiar to Anglo-Norman, arising, of course, under English influence. *W* is used for *vu* in *Boeve: wlt, wnt*, etc., and for *v* simply in *Bible Fragment, wus*, 3, 112, 526, 689, etc.

J

46. The only *j* we note here is the one of which Stimming makes an especial study;[6] that is, the inorganic *j* inserted to break hiatus, as *baier* (BADARE), *chaier* (CADERE), etc. It is written either as *y* or *i*. It is peculiar to Anglo-Norman, in that it occurs only before the accented syllable, whereas the parasitic *i* found in eastern and northeastern France appears after all vowels in all positions.

For R + J, N + J, see under the consonant R, p. 90, § 37, 3.

---

[1] Stimming, p. 219.
[3] *Ibid.* p. 220.
[5] *Boeve*, p. 220.

[2] *Ibid. Boeve*, p. 220.
[4] Schumann, p. 38.
[6] *Ibid.* pp. 237, 238.

S

47. S BEFORE A CONSONANT

We now enter upon one of the most important chapters in the history of Anglo-Norman consonants, and of Old French consonants as well, because the Anglo-Norman developments indicate to us many of the developments for general Old French. We may say, in a summary fashion, that phenomena observed in any portion of French territory seem to respond to general tendencies; only variations, of more or less importance, are peculiar to the separate dialects. Of the dialects, however, no single one is as important, probably, for the general history of the subject as is Anglo-Norman.

The main points of the question appear at once when we consider, for example, the English words *blame*, *meddle*, *forest*, which preserve to this day Anglo-Norman tendencies of centuries ago. In the first word (*blame*) we note complete disappearance of the *s* (of *blasmer*), in the second (*meddle*) we have *d* substituted for the *s* (of *mesler*), in the third (*forest*) we see the perseverance of the Latin *s*.

The first extended study of the point was that of Koritz.[1] His work was reviewed by Paris,[2] and, as usual, the master's review was, in effect, a wonderfully clear presentation of the whole subject, and subsequent grammarians[3] have had little to do beyond accepting the divisions and adopting the conclusions of Paris. The etyma showing s before a consonant must be considered in two distinct series. first, s + J, F, V; + B, D, G; L, M, N, R; second, s + P, T, C. In the first series s is voiced, in the second it is voiceless.

Of especial interest in Anglo-Norman is the history of the s before *l* and *n*, and before *t*. For s + *l* we find *sl*, *dl*, *ll*, and disappearance of *s*: *isle*, *idle*, *ille*, *ile*. For s + *n* we

---

[1] *Ueber das s vor consonant im Französischen*, Strassburg, 1885.
[2] *Rom.* XV, 614–623.
[3] Cf. Meyer-Lubke, *Gram.* I, 476, § 529 , Nyrop, *Gram.* I, 351.

find *sn, dn, gn* (*sgn, nn*), and disappearance: *disner, didner, digner,* (*disgner, areinnad*), *diner.*   For *s + t,* we find *st, ht* (*ght, sht*), and disappearance: *ostel, osaht* (*eght, oshtel*), *otel.* It is not necessary to give full examples.   Kóritz[1] cites them from eight early texts (though some of his examples are to be controlled by later editions or critiques of these texts).   In addition to the references to be found below, Stimming gives many examples from various texts.[2]

48. S BEFORE L AND N.

1. GENERAL REMARKS ON SUBSTITUTE LETTERS.   The first point to be noted with regard to every combination which we shall have to record as a substitute for *s +* a consonant (*dl, dn, gn,* etc.) is that in the case of each one there was, for a time, discussion whether the substituted letter had a phonetic value, or represented only the replacing of one silent letter by another.   The early investigators took the latter position, as a rule, as we shall see below.   Kóritz,[3] for example, considers the substitute signs as silent substitutes, and dates the disappearance of the *s +* consonant from the time when such substitutes began to be used.   This position was one which might easily have suggested itself to early students and editors (of Anglo-Norman texts) when they confronted the apparent inconsistencies in the Mss. in the transcribing of Anglo-Norman representatives of Latin words having s + consonant.   The earliest texts, both in prose and poetry, contain examples of nearly, if not quite, all possible variants.   The *Q. L. R.,* for example, has *sl, ll, dl, sn, dn, gn, nn.*   There is now no question but that these letters before the *l* and *n* signified an actual pronunciation, however unemphatic and transitory that pronunciation may have been, and that they preserve some of the stages through which *s* passed before its early disappearance, when in contact with *l* and *n.*

[1] pp, 10–18.
[2] *Boeve,* p. 224 (*dl*); p. 224 (*dn*); p. 216 (*gn*); pp. xl, liii, 225 (*st*).
[3] p. 32.

2. DL. Mall spoke emphatically of the *d* of *adne* and *medler* as indicating the silencing of the *s*. More minute study, however, soon brought out the fact that, since this *d* for *s* was present only before the dental liquids, *l* and *n* (not before *m*, for example), there must be a phonetic reason for such limitation, and the *d* came to be looked upon as a step in the complete assimilation of the *s* to the *l* (or *n*). The *s* was a voiced fricative, pronounced, doubtless, with but little energy, and it was but little separated from the voiced stop *d*, whose value (in *adne* or *medler*) may not even have been that of a complete stop, but more like English *th* in *this* [1]

The explanation just mentioned seems sufficient from a phonetic point of view; nevertheless, others have been attempted. For instance, *mesler* > *mesdler* > *medler* has been suggested.[2] [The *mesdler* here spoken of is probably to be compared with *disgner* and *oshtel*, all three being crossings in orthography; that is, *oshtel* = *ostel* + *ohtel; disgner* = *disner* + *digner; mesdler* = *mesler* + *medler*.]

Again, the following has been proposed, and by no less an authority than Foerster:[3] *sl* > *ll* > *dl; sn* > *nn* > *dn*. His idea encountered but little favor.[4]

3. LL. The usual treatment of *ll* has been that of a good illustration of consonant assimilation in French; as such, it matters little whether we adopt the stage *sl* > *ll* directly or *sl* > *dl* > *ll*. The *ll* occurs in the *Domesday Book* (*Gillebert* < *Gislibert*) and our earliest texts.[5]

We have the suggestion, new so far as Anglo-Norman is concerned, that the *ll* may represent an *l* mouillée, and much

---

[1] Cf. Mall, *Cumpoz*, pp. 88 and 90 , Behrens, *Franz. Stud.* V, 183 ; Schlosser, *Q L R.* p 73 , Paris, *Rom.* XV, 618, 620.

[2] Merwart, *Q L. R.* p. 8, f.-n. 1.

[3] *Zt.* XXII, 265, f.-n. 1.

[4] Cf. *Zt.* XXII, 513 ; *Rom.* XXVIII, 145; *Jhrsbrcht.* V, H. 2, p. 291.

[5] *Zt* IV, 556 ; VIII, 362 ; *Rom.* XV, 618 , Schlosser, *Q L. R.* p. 72.

is brought forward in favor of this view.[1] This question merits further study, and several additional circumstances will have to be considered. For example, there is this much against the old idea of assimilation; namely, that the final stage of assimilation of two consonants is usually represented by a single remaining consonant; on the other hand, Anglo-Norman has a fondness for double consonants, notably *ll* and *rr* (cf. above, p. 81). Since the supposed development of $l' < sl$ must necessarily be compared with that of $n' < sn$, the orthographic signs for the two should be compared: we find *ll* and *nn*; the latter is sometimes equivalent to *n'* (cf. p. 88). As *ll* is supposed to stand for $l' < sl$, in how far does *nn* occur for $n' < sn$? It is found in *areinnad* in Q. L. R., which is so rich in variants for $s +$ consonant.[2] Does *nn* occur for *sn* after vowels other than *i*; that is, is it used to mark assimilation too, as *ll* supposedly is? Investigation along these, among other, lines may throw new light on the point.

4. DN. The *d* here is the same as that described under $s + l$ (p. 103, 2), and all references given there apply equally well here. No English words have preserved the stage *dn*, corresponding to *dl* (*meddler*).

5. GN. Here again we must note that early scholars thought of *gn* as a mere orthographic variant of *sn*, with no phonetic value, and they discussed whether *sn* was changed to *gn* directly, or whether *sn* was first written as *n*, and this *n* then confused with *gn*.[3]

Suchier[4] called attention to the fact that in Q. L. R. *s* is

---

[1] By Walberg, *Best.* pp. lxiv, lxv. Paris makes no objection to the suggestion in his review of Walberg, *Rom.* XXIX, 590. [On line 14 of p. 590, read LXV instead of XLV.]

[2] Schlosser, p. 73.

[3] Cf. Koschwitz, *Ueberlief.* p. 27, f.-n. ; Schumann, *Camb. Psalt.* p. 49 ; Neumann, *Zt.* VIII, 383, f.-n

[4] *Zt.* I, 429 ; cf. Schlosser's rectification of Suchier's statement, Q. L. R. p. 73, f.-n. 243.

replaced by *d* or *g*, according to the consonant following the
s; speaking of *gn*, he says he thinks it equivalent to *g-n*
(that is, both pronounced), but not *n'*.

In his study of the *Q L. R.* Schlosser[1] said there was
no doubt but that the *gn* < *sn* was there equivalent to *n'*.
This idea is developed by Paris[2] in his review of Koritz, in
which Paris says that *g* is found for *s* only before *n* and
after *i*; that is, under conditions where *ign* usually represents *n'*. If *ign* for *isn* occurred in Anglo-Norman alone we
might consider it a mere graphic variant, but it is found in
regions quite diverse. It is probable that after *i*, the voiced
s before *n* developed a sound which in combination with *n*
approached *n'* (cf. below, p. 107, *str* > *istr*).

49. S BEFORE T.

At first sight, matters here seem involved. Before the
voiceless stops, *s* surely remained in early Anglo-Norman;
modern English words, like *forest, beast*, seem to point to its
consistent retention, yet, in later Anglo-Norman, not only
did the *s* certainly fall, but Anglo-Norman orthography
illustrates the stages of the fall. We shall treat of these
points below.

1. EARLY RETENTION OF S. The early monuments do
not show the silencing of the *s*. Such are the *Cumpoz*,[3]
Bestiaire,[4] *Oxf. Psalt.*,[5] and *Camb. Psalt.*[6] It thus becomes
evident that the *s* had not fallen in France at the time of
the Norman conquest, and that the consideration of *s* before
t must be different from that of *s* before *l* and *n*. Paris
places Anglo-Norman and Wallonian together as illustrating
the keeping of the *s* before *p*, *t*, and *c*.

2. FALL OF S.

a. Date. We have a famous example, for a long time
supposed to be the earliest to show the fall of the *s + t*; this

---

[1] p. 73.
[3] Mall, p 90.
[5] Harseim, p. 323.
[2] *Rom.* XV, 619.
[4] Walberg, p. lxvii
[6] Schumann, p 48

is the one furnished by the rhyme *est*: *met*, l. 882 of Philippe's *Bestiaire*. Walberg[1] proposed to shatter the force of the old example by offering the reading *s'en est* in place of *me(s)t*, which reading he adopts in his edition,[2] commenting again upon it. The new reading has not been accorded universal acceptance;[3] the objection to it, however, is based on the sense of the passage, and there seems to be no question but that the old reading is so doubtful that it carries no weight as exemplifying the fall of *s* + *t*.[4]

The *s* before *t* had certainly begun to fall in the early part of the thirteenth century, but we have direct evidence that all traces of the *s* had not been lost before the latter part of the same century. This testimony is offered by the *Orthographia Gallica*,[5] where we find the rule that when *s* is joined to *t*, it has the sound of *h*, and that *est*, *plest* should be pronounced *eght*, *pleght*. This statement reads almost like a commentary on texts near the *Orthographia* in time, as the *Chevalier, Dame et Clerc*, where we find *miht* (118), *conuht* (180), *fiht* (508), etc., and *mushter* (8), *oshtel* (27).

b. Stages. The rule of the *Orthographia Gallica* just cited, while proving the perseverance of the *s*, shows, too, one of the stages through which the *s* passed before disappearance, — the stage *h*. Neumann[6] developed this idea, based among other things on the rhymes of German poets who seem to have tried to transcribe phonetically words borrowed from the French. Kóritz[7] did not like the idea, but Neumann adhered to it,[8] and it is génerally accepted now. The *s* certainly did not disappear suddenly, the *h* was obviously not a mere sign of the lengthening of the preceding vowel, but represents one of the many series of changes *s* may have

---

[1] *Rom.* XXVII, 146.   [2] *Best.* p. lxvii.

[3] Cf. *Rom.* XXIX, 591 ; *Jhrsbrcht.* V, H. 2, p. 291 (Vising).

[4] Cf. Vising, *l.c.*, and *Rom.* XV, 621.   [5] pp. 8 and 49.

[6] *Zur Laut- und Flexionslehre des Altfranzösischen*, Heilbronn, 1878, pp. 106–109.

[7] *Svor Cons.* p. 34.   [8] *Litblt.* VI, 243.

undergone before disappearance. Neumann himself does not claim long life for the *h* stage.[1]

3. ENGLISH WORDS WITH ST. If *s* + *t* did undoubtedly disappear in Anglo-Norman, how are we to account for English words like *feast, forest,* where *s* is kept? For this we have two suggestions. that of Behrens,[2] that the quiescence of the *s* was gradual and not completed till the fourteenth century; and that of Paris,[3] that the English borrowed such words from French before *s* was silenced, or else that the pronunciation of the *s* was weakened ("ébranlée") at one time, and afterwards strengthened again ("raffermie").

4. STR>ISTR. It is worth noting in connection with the keeping of *s* + *t* in the early texts and in connection with the supposed palatalizing influence of the *s* on a following *l* or *n* (cf. above, p. 104) that Horning in his suggestive note on *s* + consonant > *y*[4] explains *cheveistre* < CAPISTRUM in the *Camb. Psalt* as follows. in order to facilitate the enunciation of the group, the *s* was pronounced softly and thus developed a *y* out of the group.

5. INORGANIC S + T. It goes without saying that we find examples of *s* inserted before a *t* where it has no etymological right, and from the time of our earliest texts (*mercist, nuist, toste,* etc).[5] Cf. below, p. 121, 3, b where this *s* appears in certain verb forms.

GENERAL SUMMARY (48-49)

As has already been brought out, the date of the fall of the *s* before liquids, and that before *t* are quite independent of each other. In the case of the liquids, Anglo-Norman preserves in its orthography some of the phonetic phenomena

---

[1] Cf. here Paris, *Rom* XV, 621 ; Behrens, *Franz Stud.* V, 183, and the confirmation of the theory presented (incidentally) by F. Wulff in *Mém. Philol. présent à G. Paris par élèv suéd* , Stockholm, 1889, p. 256.   [2] *l. c.*

[3] *Rom.* XV, 622, f.-n.   [4] *Zt.* XXIIII, 414

[5] References and examples, Stimming, *Boeve,* 227, 228.

attendant upon the fall before *l* and *n*; consequently we may not say more than that the quiescence of the *s* before *l* and *n* was taking place in French at the time of the Norman Conquest. In the case of the other liquids, and the other consonants of the first series formulated by Paris (cf. p. 101²), the fall had taken place before the Conquest. Before *t* the fall is much later, instances are found for the first part of the thirteenth century; a trace of the *s* (I refer to *h*) is present in the latter part of that century, and the general fall was probably not complete till the fourteenth century. The strong hold that *st* once had in Anglo-Norman is reflected in English derivatives like *feast* and *tempest*.

50. S INTERVOCALIC.

Anglo-Norman writers were inconsistent in their use of *s* and *ss*, employing them indiscriminately for the voiced and voiceless *s*. A favorite method of indicating voiceless *s* was by the use of *sc*; for the same purposes we find *z* and *c*, though both of these occur for voiced *s* also.[1]

51. S FINAL.

It is very evident that final *s* and *z* may have the same value in Anglo-Norman (that of *s*) from the earliest time.[2] A remarkable exception is presented by Guillaume de Berneville, who observes an absolute distinction between final *s* and *z*, while all traces of *t* and *d* final after accented vowels are lost. For example, *-as*, *-es*, *-eis*, *-us* never rhyme with *-az*, *-ez*, *-eiz*, *-uz*.[3] Other similar cases are cited by Stimming,[4] who supposes that the old value of the *z* (that is, *ts*) may have been preserved in some instances, as is evident from English proper names containing *Fitz*.

---

[1] Examples and references, Stimming, *Boeve*, 224, 228; cf. *Zt.* XIII, 86.

[2] Some general references here are, Stimming, *Boeve*, pp. 225, 230; Walberg, *Best.* pp. lxiv, xcii; Meyer-Lubke, *Gram.* I, 505, § 561; II, 239, § 173; Vising, *Étude*, p. 95.

[3] Paris edition, p. xxxii.   [4] *Boeve*, p. 230.

1. MISCELLANEOUS. Several orthographic confusions may be noted here. In the *Arundel Psalt.*, where *s* follows a consonant, we have both *s* and *z* written. *oilsz, jursz, queransz*,[1] etc.; many more examples might be cited; we find also *seiesz* (verb),[2] and *-stz* in *mercistz, eslistz*.[3] In the *Camb. Psalt.* we find an example of *x* for *s* in *reix*, V, 1. The *d* for *s* in the same text is a variation of the *d* for *z* already referred to above (p. 96): *flechisums nod genuilz* (XCIV, 6). We note one example of *t* for *s* in *Vie Gregoire, vert* (l. 2017).

---

[1] *Zt.* XI, 517, 519, 521. [2] *Ibid* XII, 9.

[3] *Ibid* XII, 9, 10.

MORPHOLOGY

DEFINITE ARTICLE

52. 1. GENERAL. In the *Psalters* and the *Lois Guillaume* we find the regular Old French forms. *Li* is not apocopated in the *Psalters* (*Oxf.* and *Camb.*) ; it is in *Q. L. R.* and *Lois Guillaume*, though only in the construction *l'um* (or its variants, *l'em*, etc.).[1]

2. ACCUSATIVE FOR NOMINATIVE. The first examples of *le* and *les* as nominatives that I have noted in our texts are in Chardri, where they occur by the side of the regular *li*, which is used with certain restrictions, *le* and *les* being the more frequent.[2] In *Auban*, too, the latter are found, though not as frequently as *li*.[3]

On the use of the nominative article with an accusative noun, see below, p. 113, § 54, 1.

3. CONFUSION OF MASCULINE AND FEMININE ARTICLES. The use of the masculine *le* for feminine *la* is old in Anglo-Norman, dating from the *Bestiaire*[4] (*le gambe, le allegorie*) and *Q. L. R.*, and becoming more and more frequent toward the end of the Anglo-Norman period. The use of the *le* seems to have arisen in those cases in which the vowel (of *la*) could be elided. However, detailed study of this point will doubtless reveal irregularities for whose origin no such explanation exists.

4. LU. Two interesting forms of the article are *lu* and *lui*. The older of the two is doubtless *lu*, variant of the accusative *le*, though it is difficult, in some cases, to distin-

---

[1] Schlosser, p. 43 ; Matzke, p. 41.   [2] Koch, p. xxxviii.
[3] Uhlemann, p. 621.   [4] Walberg, p. lxxiv.

guish when *lu* is an article and when a variant of the pro-
nominal form *lui* *Lu* is found in the *Arundel Psalt.*: *en
lu seignur*,[1] in *Quatre Livres des Rois*,[2] in Fantosme (1. 290),
in *Brandan*,[3] and it is made the subject of a special note by
Meyer in connection with Angier.[4] It is found in *Vie St.
Thomas*, too (II, 34, *il e lu roi*), and often in the *Pèlerinage*.

This *lu* has been noted especially as the equivalent of *del*,
that is, the genitive. It occurs in *Auban* (62, *as nosces lu
ber*, 991, *le cors lu martir*),[5] often in the *Pèlerinage* (882, *la
femme lu rei*, 852, *la fille lu rei*), and a number of times in
the *Vie St. Thomas* (III, 19, 118; IV, 100). There is, probably, nothing distinctive about such usage, it corresponding
to general Old French, *as nosces le ber*, etc.

5. Lui. Even if *lu* be the original form, it was never
used with the frequency which we note for *lui*. *Lui* can be
graphic variant, in Anglo-Norman, of either *lu* or *li* (cf. p. 80,
§ 33, 1). Consequently we find *lui* as nominative and accusative singular, and nominative plural. Examples are given
by Stimming,[6] to which are to be added some from the *Pèlerinage* (788, *la gent lui rei*), from Angier[7] (*lui vilein*), and
from the *Apocalypse* (65, p. 202, *lui dreins*). It will be seen
that most of the texts cited are of a comparatively late date,
Gaimar and Angier being the exceptions.

Stimming cites instances of *lui* as feminine singular (from
two texts).

6. Miscellaneous. In addition to *lu*, mentioned above,
we note the following forms from the *Arundel Psalt.* which
are not cited from any other text, as far as I know: *leu* (*en
leu cuer*); *lau* (*lau tue glorie*); *leis* (*leis peissuns*).[8] In each
of these cases the extra vowel in the form of the article
seems to anticipate the corresponding vowel in the word
following the article.

---

[1] *Zt.* XII, 21.　　　　　　　[2] Ed. Michel, p. 434.
[3] Brekke, p. 48.　　　　　　　[4] *Rom.* XII, 199
[5] Uhlemann, p. 577.　　　　　[6] *Boeve*, p. xii.
[7] Cloran, p. 57.　　　　　　　[8] *Zt* XII, 31; XI, 529, 520.

ADJECTIVES

53. The only point we have to note here — beyond referring to forms like *vifs* (whose history is the same as that of nouns like *colps*, p. 113, 2) and beyond recording that in Anglo-Norman we must not expect a masculine or feminine noun to be preceded or followed consistently by the corresponding masculine or feminine form of adjective or participle — is the early appearance of feminines of the GRANDIS, FOLLIS type with an -*e*. The *Cumpoz, Oxf. Psalt.*, and *Brandan* show *fole, forte, sueve, ardante*, etc., by the side of the older *fort, ardant, suef*, etc.[1] The new feminines abound in Angier: *quele, tale, passante*, etc.[2]

For the form *tuit* used in the singular as well as plural, cf. above, p. 68, § 21, 4. In *Vie St. Edmond*, 2930, we have one of the rare examples of *beleisur*.[3]

NOUNS

54. We shall treat here of the substitution of accusative for nominative; of the peculiar forms *nefs, verms*, etc.; and refer to some miscellaneous points.

1. ACCUSATIVE FOR NOMINATIVE. The origin of the reduction of the declension from two cases (nominative and accusative) to one (accusative) is usually associated with Anglo-Norman; the justice of the tradition is derived, not from the non-appearance of the phenomenon at an early date elsewhere than in Anglo-Norman, but from the consistency that marks the reduction in Anglo-Norman. To illustrate our meaning, we find that in Norman, for example, traces of the change are to be detected already before the year 1180 in *Roman du Mont Saint Michel*, and the change is marked in Guillaume le Clerc (first part of the fourteenth century); but, on the other hand, it is never met with in Wace (1125–1174).[4] In Anglo-Norman, on the contrary,

---

[1] Cf. Mall, p. 106; Hammer, p. 114; Brekke, pp. 40, 44; Meyer-Lubke, *Gram.* II, 86, § 60.　　[2] *Rom.* XII, 199.

[3] Cf. Meyer-Lubke, *Gram.* II, 93, § 66.　　[4] Paris, *Vie St. Gilles*, p. xxi.

examples are found in an uninterrupted succession; for example, the *Cumpoz*,[1] *Lois Guillaume*,[2] *Oxf. Psalt.*,[3] *Camb. Psalt.*,[4] *Brandan*,[5] Angier,[6] Chardri,[7] *Vie St. Thomas*,[8] *Boeve*,[9] *Amadas*,[10] *Chevalier, Dame et Clerc*,[11] *Auban*,[12] *Donner*,[13] etc.

The nature and manner of this change are studied by Koschwitz[14] for the *Oxf. Psalt.* Mall, too (*l.c.*), studies irregularities such as nominative article or adjective with accusative noun. We must not forget that the opposite process of the one referred to occurs; that is, the use of nominative for accusative.[15]

For the time order of this phenomenon in Anglo-Norman as compared with other dialects we have several statements.[16]

Brekke[17] attempted statistics to show that the author of the *Brandan* was more careful than Philippe de Thaun in his use of the cases; Brekke resents having his author classed with Philippe in this connection. A similar line of investigation, that is, trying to draw deductions as to purity of language from the comparative frequency with which two given authors avail themselves of a given phenomenon, has never been followed to any extent.

2. NEFS, SACS, COLPS, ETC. These, and similar forms, are very frequent in Anglo-Norman, for example, *Oxf. Psalt.*,[18] *Camb. Psalt.*,[19] *Q. L. R.*,[20] *Brandan*,[21] Chardri,[22] *Boeve*,[23] and *Auban*.[24] They do not occur in the *Cumpoz*,[25]

---

[1] Mall, pp. 97–100.
[2] Matzke, p. 1.
[3] *Zt.* I, 569; II, 485.
[4] *Ibid.* I, 569.
[5] Brekke, p. 81.
[6] Meyer, p 198, Cloran, p. 54.
[7] *Zt.* III, 594.
[8] Meyer, p. xxviii.
[9] Stimming, p. xiv.
[10] *Zt.* XIII, 86.
[11] *Rom* I, 72.
[12] Uhlemann, p 613.
[13] *Rom.* XXV, 532
[14] *Zt.* II, 485
[15] *Ibid.* II, 488.
[16] Meyer-Lübke, *Gram.* II, 39, § 25, Such. *Français et Provençal*, p 163; (in) Grober's *Grundriss*, I, 638, Warnke, *Zt.* IV, 234.
[17] p. 81.
[18] *Zt.* I, 560.
[19] Schumann, p 46, &c.
[20] Schlosser, pp 66, 80.
[21] Hammer, p. 108; Brekke, pp 25–30.
[22] Koch, p. xxxiv.
[23] Stimming, pp. xiv, 181, 220.
[24] Uhlemann, p. 598.
[25] Mall, p. 105.

I

with the exception of *verms,* nor need we expect to find them
to the exclusion of *nes, sas,* etc., in the other texts.

This set of words must be studied in connection with the
question of the value of final *s,* which, apparently, was not
stable.   The early adoption of the accusative for the nominative probably impressed the form of the accusative on
the minds of our scribes, and the nominative, under consideration, doubtless represented to them the traditional *-s* (of the
nominative) added to this accusative.   The scribes insert
nefs, sacs, colps, etc., even in rhymes (as Chardri, *Boeve,*
Auban), but thereby again demonstrate uncertainty in the
use of their own language, because evidence is against the
pronunciation of the *p, b, v, c + s* in rhyme.

3. MISCELLANEOUS.   I append here some references on
the following points: confusion of genders;[1] neuter nominatives, *jugement, conseil,* etc.;[2] formation of compound nouns;[3]
masculine *pere* type with *s;*[4] feminine *fleur* type without *s;*[5]
distinction between *ans* and *anz, fils* and *filz.*[6]   We note, too,
further instances of the uncertainty of our scribes, in that
they sometimes omit an etymological post-tonic *e* before flexional *s* (as *colurs* = COLUBRAS, *pers* = PETRAS), and again
they insert an inorganic *e* (as *coupes* = *colps, manteles* =
mantels, etc.).[7]

PERSONAL PRONOUNS

55. FIRST PERSON.

1. JE AND JOE.   Our older texts offer nothing striking
here.   Already in Chardri *je,* as tonic form, rhymes in *é:*
pri je : marche, demant je : cunge, etc.[8]   The form *joe* is made
the subject of a note by Paris in his edition of the *Donnei.*[9]
He says that he had usually regarded *joe* as a variant of *jo*

---

[1] Meyer-Lübke, *Gram.* II, 450, § 302.   [2] *Ibid.* II, 13, § 8.
[3] *Ibid.* II, 630, § 547.   [4] *Ibid.* II, 33, § 22.
[5] *Ibid.* II, 32, § 21 (bis).   [6] *Litblt.* VI, 116.
[7] Stimming, *Boeve,* pp. 182, 183.   [8] Sturzinger, *Orth. Gall.* p. 45.
[9] *Rom.* XXV, 532, f.-n. 6.

or *jue*, but that in the *Donnei* we have to suppose a dissyllabic pronunciation, *joé*. He refers to *joe* as an Anglo-Norman form. The same occurs, for example, in the *Bible Fragment*, line 793,[1] and *coe* is often used in the same text, as 116, 137, 194, etc. (cf. *tue*, below, § 56, 1).

2. Mɪ. This form is cited by Vising,[2] who says it is equivalent to *mei* (*moi*) in Fantosme and Adgar. It occurs also in Picard, Norman, and Lorraine, and is doubtless the *mi* referred to by Meyer-Lübke[3] as derived from ᴍɪʜɪ. It is late and rare in Anglo-Norman, more frequent elsewhere.

56. SECOND PERSON.

1. Tu ᴀɴᴅ Vous. An interesting syntactical phenomenon arises here; that is, the confusion of *tu* and *vous*, the two being employed without any apparent distinction in meaning in one and the same sentence. Suchier speaks of this point.[4]

The form *tue* occurs in *Arundel Psalt.* ;[5] if not a corrupt reading, it is worthy of attention in connection with *jue*, and recalls the early Italian *tue*.[6]

2. Ous. In *Donnei*, 816, 973, we find *jous* (= *je vous*) and *quideus* (= *cuidiez vous*). Similar forms occur in Chardri and *Ipomedon*. The *ous* for *vous* is not uncommon in Old French.[7]

57. THIRD PERSON.

Here I shall speak of the use of the tonic for the atonic forms, and of the general confusion of forms, singular and plural, masculine and feminine.

---

[1] *Rom.* XVI, 206.   [2] *Litblt.* V, 68   [3] *Gram.* II, 102, § 75.

[4] *Auban*, p. 8.   Cf. additional references in *Zt.* V, 164.

[5] *Zt.* XI, 521.   [6] Cf. Meyer-Lubke, *Ital. Gram.* § 148. (In Italian translation, § 88.)

[7] Cf. *Rom.* XXV, 533.   Tobler's original article on the point is in *Zt.* VIII, 496 , additions to this were made by Behrens, *Zt.* XIII, 408. Cf. also, Meyer-Lubke, *Gram.* I, 379, § 429; II, 110, § 78, and 408, § 325.

1. Tonic Instead of Atonic Forms. This phenomenon, quite common throughout Old French, is very marked in Anglo-Norman from the time of the earliest texts; as *Cumpoz, Oxf. Psalt., Arundel Psalt., Alexis*, etc.: *jetent sei, sei pastierent, jo toi pri*, etc. (It goes without saying that the confusion is not confined to the third person.) Koch, in his edition of Chardri, made distinctions (and determined his readings thereby) according to the position, or rather significance, of the given pronoun in the sentence; but in this he was criticized by Mussafia.[1] In Angier[2] we find that the use of atonic forms is accounted a rarity.

2. Confusion of Forms in the Singular.

a. Masculine, *lu = lui, lu = lo.* We have already referred (p. 110, 4) to *lu*; both *lu* and *li* (which occurs here as throughout Old French) are regular phonetic reductions of *lui* in Anglo-Norman (cf. p. 80, § 33, 1). *Lu* occurs frequently in Chardri and Angier: *quant il lu vit, a lu apparut*, etc. Any syntactical principle indicating a preference for *lui* or for *lu* or for *li* is not apparent; Cloran[3] suggests that in the *Dialogues Gregoire lu* after prepositions is rare.

We must note, too, that *lu* is used for accusative *lo* in the same texts in which *lu* is found for *lui*. Koschwitz[4] suggested a distinction between Anglo-Norman *lu* and general French *le*, saying that *lu* goes directly back to *lo* (that is, it is a variant of *lo*), while *le* is derived from *lo* through the stage *lö*. For *is = il*, see below (3, a) under plural forms.

b. Feminine. I give here some references on the following points: use of *lui, le,* and *la* as equivalents of feminine dative *li*; use of *le* for *la*, accusative;[5] for *le = ele*, see just below, under *lei = ele; el = ele* is found in the twelfth century in Norman and Anglo-Norman.[6] For the correspond-

---

[1] Cf. Koch, p. xxxix; *Zt.* III, 596. [2] Cf. Meyer, p. 199; Cloran, p. 56.
[3] p. 57. [4] *Ueberlieferung*, p. 25. [5] Stimming, *Boeve*, p. xxii.
[6] Cf. Meyer-Lübke, *Gram.* II, 109, § 78; Such. *Français et Provençal*, p. 136; Walberg, *Best.*, p. lxxiv.

ing plural *els = eles,* see below; *lei* for *la* is cited by Cloran[1] for the *Dialogues Gregoire; de lei soccoure,* etc.; a variant of this *lei* in the same text is *le: en le entrerent,* etc.

3. CONFUSION OF FORMS IN THE PLURAL.

a. *is = il.* *is* occurs for both singular and plural — for *il* and *ils.* So far as I know it is peculiar to Angier: *qu'is eit, qu'is orent,* etc. It occurs in both his *Vie* and his *Dialogues Gregoire.*[2]

b. *es = eles.* This is given for Angier by Meyer as the feminine corresponding to the *is* just mentioned; the only instance cited is, *deu donst qu'es puessent;* Cloran does not cite it for the *Dialogues.*

c. *il = eles.* This usage is referred to by Suchier[3] as occurring often in Anglo-Norman.

d. *els = eles.* This corresponds to *el = elle* mentioned above.

e *les = lis,* dative plural. References for this peculiarity are given by Stimming,[4] who attributes the use (and that of *lur* as accusative) to English influence; the same occurs in Wallonian and Picard, however.[5]

DEMONSTRATIVE PRONOUNS

58. Here we note the following: *cel* and *cest* occur early for the nominative in Norman and Anglo-Norman;[6] the neuter *cel,* particularly in the locution *puet cel estre* is confined, for the most part, to these two dialects;[7] the neuter *ceo* occurs often as an adjective in *Boeve (ceo traitur),* but this is a peculiarity of texts of comparatively late date;[8] *ist,* masculine, and *iste,* feminine, seldom found in general Old French, occur frequently in *Dialogues Gregoire.*[9]

[1] p. 58. [2] Meyer, p. 199, Cloran, p. 55.

[3] *Zt.* IV, 419, cf. Meyer-Lübke, *Gram* II, 110, § 78.

[4] *Boeve,* p. xxii.

[5] Cf. Meyer-Lübke, *Gram.* II, 115, § 83, and Vising, *Zt fr. Spr. u Lit* XXII, H 2, p. 25. [6] Meyer-Lübke, *Gram* II, 132, § 96.

[7] *Ibid* II, 135, § 98; Walberg, *Best* p. lxxxv.

[8] Stimming, *Boeve,* p. xxv, cf. Vising, ref. above. [9] Cloran, p. 57.

POSSESSIVE PRONOUNS

59. There is little that is characteristic to be noted here; variations are confined for the most part to the forms of the feminine.

1. FEMININE. Frequently we find *mei = meie, tu = tue*, which illustrate the loss of post-tonic *e* (cf. p. 63, § 18, 1, a); these forms are frequent in the *Psalters*, especially the *Camb. Psalt.* (as XXX, 16, *en la tu main;* LVI, 7, *mei aneme*), also in *Arundel Psalt., moi oreille, mei ureisun.*[1]

We have already spoken of the feminine article *le* for *la* (p. 110, 3); we find the possessives *sa* and *ma* replaced by *se* and *me* in our earliest texts, as *Camb. Psalt.* LXI, 11, *se ovre; Arundel Psalt., se felonie,*[2] and similar cases in the *Q. L. R.*[3]

2. MISCELLANEOUS FORMS. We note in the *Camb. Psalt. mis, tis* (XXVI, 4, 9, 16, etc.) constantly where the *Oxf. Psalt.* has *mes, tes.* The former shows also *meins* (XII, 4), *mieins* (XVII, 34), and *nod* for *nos* (cf. above, p. 109, § 51, 1). In the *Arundel Psalt.* we note *mens, meiens, muen, ten.*[4] In *Vie Gregoire* we note *sis* (64, 655) and *soue* (1730, 1741).

RELATIVE PRONOUNS

60. Our texts offer nothing extraordinary here; *ki* early makes a place for itself beside *qui* or *chi;* it is found in *Cumpoz, Lois Guillaume,* the *Psalters,* and *Q. L. R.* with gradually increasing frequency. In the accusative *ke* for *que* appears as early as the *Camb. Psalt.* and *Q. L. R.*[5] Chardri uses *ke,* as well as *ki,* for the nominative; Koch changed the *ke* to *ki* in many cases (in which procedure Mussafia did not agree with him).[6] In *Boeve,* the usual form for both cases is *ke.*

---

[1] Cf. *Zt.* I, 569; XII, 17, 48; XI, 515.   [2] *Zt.* XI, 519.
[3] Schlosser, p. 8.   [4] *Zt.* XI, 516, 533; XII, 5, 17.
[5] Matzke, p. li; Such. *Litblt.* XXII, 120, f.-n. 2.
[6] Koch, p. xxxix; *Zt.* III, 595.

VERBS

61. INTERCHANGE OF CONJUGATIONS.

This process is a most frequent one in Anglo-Norman. It is difficult to detect any underlying principle, because there is hardly any change that does not work two ways In Anglo-Norman, as in general French, the first weak conjugation (*-er* < *-are*) seems to exercise the greatest power of attraction, though, as we shall see, it sometimes suffers losses to other conjugations.

1. -EIR > -ER. We have here a change that is characteristic of our dialect, as compared with French of the continent; it seems to have originated in Anglo-Norman, and about the middle of the twelfth century.[1] The change of conjugation affected the infinitive most of all; four infinitives were altered the earliest of all, setting the example to the rest; these were *aveir, poeir, saveir, voleir* > *aver, poer, saver, voler*.[2] We notice *voer* (for *veeir*, VIDERE) already in the *Arundel Psalt.*,[3] and the same occurs as *voier* (: *travaillier*) in *Vie Gregoire*, 351.

2. -RE, -IR > -ER. This change is later than the one first mentioned, and illustrates the strength which the *-er* conjugation had acquired in Anglo-Norman, by virtue of the older change (*-eir* > *-er*). We find *tener, repenter, attender,* and the like, in the course of the thirteenth century.[4]

3. -ER > -RE. We note *gettre, leetre* (< *laitier*), *luttre* in *Boeve, Auban,* and *Bozon*.[5] Cf. above, p. 91, b.

---

[1] Cf. *Litbit* IV, 311; Such. *Fr. et Prov.* p. 23; Meyer-Lubke, *Gram.* II, 158, § 117; Stimming, *Boeve*, p. xxviii.

[2] Cf. here Paul Meyer in *Rom.* XVIII, 626, and his long note on the point in his edition of Bozon, p. lxii This note treats also of other irregularities in the Anglo-Norman conjugation.

[3] *Zt* XII, 13, 23.

[4] Cf. Meyer-Lubke, *Gram.* II, 158, § 117, Such *Auban*, p. 48.

[5] Cf. Meyer-Lubke, *Gram.* II, 167, § 124; Such. *Auban*, p. 41, Stimming, *Boeve*, p. xxix; Paul Meyer, *Bozon*, p. lxiv.

4. -ER > -IR. We find *donir, demorir, mangir* (*Otinel*, 26), and the like.[1]

5. -IER > -IR. The change in conjugation here affects more especially the infinitive, the third plural preterite, and the past participle: *lessir, froissirent, fichi.*[2]

6. -OIR AND -DRE. Anglo-Norman, too, furnishes examples of these varying forms. Already in the *Q. L. R.* we find *manoir* and *maindre.*[3]

62. PRESENT INDICATIVE.

1. FIRST PERSON SINGULAR.

a. -e. Our texts offer nothing remarkable here, and from the point of view of time no fixed line of demarcation may be drawn between those texts showing -e (as supporting vowel or analogical) and those not having it. It is present in the *Brandan,*[4] while Chardri, later and careless in his grammar, has no -e[5] (*pens, merveil, eim,* etc.), nor has *Auban*[6] nor Guillaume de Berneville.[7] *Boeve* shows -e in the first person present of the first weak conjugation, but usually omits it for the third.[8]

b. -c. Quite a number of cases of this ending are to be noted in Anglo-Norman, first of all in the *Cumpoz,*[9] *Arundel Psalt.* (*venche*),[10] and *Brandan.*[11] In Angier it is frequent; Cloran[12] cites *aourc* (ADORO), *comanc, conseilc, arc* (ARDEO), *tienc, perc* (PERDO), *regierc, serc,* etc., also *rench* and *renconch* (*recont*); in the *Vie Gregoire* I note *renc* (1843), *conmanc* (1950), *pramec* (1100). In *Boeve* we have *renc.*[13] In still later texts I note *Otinel* (*tienc,* 12), *Mélanges*[14] (*senk, pleink*), *Bible Frag-*

---

[1] Cf. Meyer-Lubke, *Gram.* II, 164, § 121; Stimming, *Boeve,* **xxix.**

[2] Cf. Such. *Auban,* p. 47; *Zt.* II, 343; *Rom.* XXVI, 88, f.-n.

[3] Meyer-Lubke, *Gram.* II, 172, § 127.

[4] Meyer-Lubke, *Gram.* II, 189, § 136.

[5] *Zt.* III, 596.   [6] Uhlemann, p. 622.

[7] Paris, p. xviii.   [8] Stimming, p. xxvi.

[9] Mall, p. 110.   [10] *Zt.* XII, 36.

[11] Brekke, p. 55.   [12] p. 59.

[13] Stimming, p. **xxix.**   [14] *Rom.* IV, 376, 377.

ment (venc, 825). The extent of this phenomenon and the character of some of the examples indicate that we may not have to do here merely with an orthographic interchange of final *t* and *c* (cf. above, p. 97, c).

2. SECOND PERSON SINGULAR.

a. *-z.* Meyer-Lubke[1] calls attention to a phenomenon that is encountered particularly in Anglo-Norman texts; in verbs whose stems end in labials, as *deveir, mover,* or *beivre,* the *s* of the second person is replaced by *z,* as *Cumpoz, deiz; Brandan, moz,* etc.

b. *-is.* The second person in *-is* is sometimes found, consequent upon the substitution in orthography of post-tonic *i* for *e* (cf. above, p. 65, 3).

3. THIRD PERSON SINGULAR.

a. Here we have to consider the question of the *t* (of *-et*). Merwart[2] gives statistics as to what verbs and tenses do or do not show the *t* in *Q. L. R.,* and makes reference to the discussions of Mall, Paris, Koschwitz, etc. Hammer[3] studies the question for the *Brandan,* and says that his text and the *Cumpoz* betray the same state of affairs: the *t* remains as a rule, may fall for the sake of the rhyme, but elision never occurs in consequence.[4] For Guillaume de Berneville, Paris finds a dozen examples of the retention of the *t* (indicative of first conjugation, subjunctive of others).[5] In a foot-note he quotes from Suchier,[6] to the effect that the elision of the *-e* did not take place in the verse until some time after the *t* had ceased to be pronounced.

b. *st = t.* The forms *dist, fest, vest* (VADIT, as *Vie St. Edmond* of Pyramus, line 1362, *vest, lest*), *dust* (DEBUIT), *cunust, morust,* are to be explained by a rule recorded in the *Orthographia Gallica,*[7] which says that in the present and preterite an *s* must be inserted between the vowels *e, i, o, u,* and the *t.*[4] The phenomenon is encountered already in Gaimar.

[1] *Gram.* II, 239, § 173.   [2] *Q L R.* p. 3.   [3] p 103.
[4] Cf. Mall, p. 109 ; Brekke, p. 56.   [5] p. xix.
[6] *Reimpredigt,* p. xxxiii.   [7] p 8.   [8] Cf. *Litblt.* VI, 116.

4. FIRST PERSON PLURAL. Here we refer to the statement already made (cf. above, p. 83) as to the early identity of *m* and *n* in the endings *-ums, -uns* (*-oms, -ons*), which rhyme together already in the *Cumpoz*.

5. SECOND PERSON PLURAL.

-et (*-ed*) = *-ez*. This peculiar form is found in the *Camb. Psalt.*[1] (*devet, pernet, entendet, corned, seied*); in the *Arundel Psalt.*[2] (*adoret, aprimet, pabitet*); *Brandan*[3] (*seet, prenget*); *Chev. Dame Clerc, freiet*, 553, and *Pèlerinage* (*huniset*, 721). The confusion of *t* (*d*) and *z* has already been considered (cf. above, p. 96); it is entirely orthographic in Anglo-Norman, and in that respect peculiar to our dialect.

6. THIRD PERSON PLURAL. We have to note here the ending *-únt* (cf. above, post-tonic *e*, p. 65, 3), and an oxytone accentuation (to be noted later for the imperfect indicative and subjunctive). Examples for this latter I have observed only in the corrupt *Apocalypse;* here in two instances we see *blasphement : habitant* (710), *portent : seint* (SANCTUM, 800). Often we find the present ending in *-únt*, as a rule to rhyme with *sunt* or *unt*; for example, *signifiunt : sunt* (73), *habitunt : sunt* (960), etc. (frequently).

63. PRESENT SUBJUNCTIVE.

1. FORMS IN *-GE* (*augez = aillez, garge = garde, perge = perde, prengez = preniez*, etc.). Similar forms are very popular in Anglo-Norman. A few references are: *Camb. Psalt.*[5] (*aherged*), *Arundel Psalt.*[6] (*auge*), Angier,[7] Chardri,[8] Boeve,[9] and *Apocalypse* (*auges*, 236).

2. FIRST AND SECOND PERSON SINGULAR. The early appearance of the (analogical or the supporting) *-e* here is characteristic of Anglo-Norman as compared with conti-

---

[1] *Zt.* I, 570.   [2] *Ibid.* XII, 15, 23, 48.

[3] Cf. Brekke, p. 56; *Ltblt.* VI, 371.

[4] Meyer-Lübke, *Gram.* II, 196, § 138.   [5] *Ibid.* 227, § 163.

[6] *Zt.* XII, 35.   [7] Meyer, p. 200; Cloran, p. 59.

[8] Koch, p. xl.   [9] Stimming, p. xxxi.

nental dialects; it is especially prevalent in the first and second persons.[1] It is found in the *Psalters* and the *Q. L R.* (cf, on the contrary, the third person *deliurt* < *delivrer* in the latter text). The *-e* is the exception in the *Lois Guillaume*,[2] and in some later texts, like Guillaume de Berneville and *Auban*, it does not appear.[3] The examples from *Boeve* illustrate the distinction between the first and second persons as compared with the third; forms without *-e* are confined to the third person.[4]

3. THIRD PERSON SINGULAR. We have just considered the late establishment of *-e* in this person. The history of the final *-t* is the same as that of *t* in the corresponding form of the indicative. Some circular combinations result from the absence of the *-e* after palatal stems; for example, *Oxf. Psalt. ceist* (*chercher*), *esculurst* (*esculurgier*), *Camb. Psalt. juszt* (*juger*), *cerche*, *juge*, etc., occur, too, however.[5]

64. IMPERFECT INDICATIVE.

The points of interest here are confined, for the most part, to the first weak conjugation.

1 OLDEST FORMS. These were *owe* or *oue*, found in the *Psalters* and the *Q L. R* ; in the third singular the post-tonic *-e* is dropped, *out* being the regular form [6] By the side of *owe*, *oue* appear *oe*, *ot*, *oent* in the *Camb. Psalt.*,[7] though they become general only in later texts These are to be considered as further developments out of *owe*, *oue*, and not *vice versa*.[8] The *-ue*, *-ut* where found [9] are doubtless variants of the *-oe*, *-ot*, *-oue*, *-out*, due to the scribes (cf above, p. 73)

2. -EIE, -OIE. The introduction of these in place of *-oue*, *-oe*, did not begin in western French territory as early as in

---

[1] Cf. Meyer-Lubke, *Gram.* II, 207, § 146 ; *Lublt.* V, 70.

[2] Matzke, p. li. [3] Uhlemann, p 622.

[4] Stimming, p. xxvii. [5] Meyer-Lubke, *Gram* II, 221, § 157.

[6] Such. *Gram* p. 31. [7] Fichte, pp. 24, 25

[8] Cf Mall, *Cumpoz*, pp. 66, 67 ; Lucking, *Aeltst Fr Mund.* p. 210.

[9] Cf. Stimming, *Boeve*, p. 189.

other parts,[1] and consequently it is not a characteristic of our first texts. In *Q. L. R.* -*eit* occurs (*guardeit, passeit*) but only in five cases as compared with 105 instances in which -*out* is retained.[2] The *rujowe* (*rujir*) of the *Oxf. Psalt.*, and the *enquerrout* of Chardri illustrate the prevalence of -*oue*.

A favorite method of studying the beginnings of the process of substitution has been that of noting the rhyming of -*oue* with -*oie* (-*eie*). Difficulties are encountered in several directions: some texts will rhyme the imperfects of a given conjugation only with imperfects of the same conjugation, as Guillaume de Berneville,[3] for example. Again, on account of the possibility of choosing from variant readings, what one editor claims as a rhyme of -*out*: -*eit* may be discarded by another student of the same text. For example, Kupfer-schmidt[4] noted the rhyme *despendeit*: *soldout* for Gaimar; Vising[5] rejected the same. (In another place, however, Vising cites four cases of the rhyme *out*: *eit* in Gaimar's *Havelok*.[6])

The first detailed study of the point is that of Suchier,[7] who considers the usage of five (minor) texts. Evidently the substitution was not universal among poets in the thirteenth century, though the tendency toward general adoption of -*eie* is to be noted from the beginning of that century and gradually becomes accentuated. Angier uses -*ot* and -*eit* in the singular, but -*oient* always in the plural.[8]

3. -EINT. This ending (for -*eient*), an example of the loss of post-tonic *e* (cf. above, p. 63), is very usual in Anglo-Norman: *esgardeint, soleint* (Chardri, *Jos.* 1158, *Pet. Plet,* 474), *poreint* (*Pèlerinage,* 511). Examples abound in manuscripts executed during and after the thirteenth century.[9] In the *Apocalypse* we find -*eint* rhyming with *ceint, forment,*

---

[1] Meyer-Lubke, *Gram.* II, 323, § 258.   [2] Merwart, p. 13.
[3] Paris, p. xxxiii.   [4] p. 417.   [5] *Étude*, p. 103.
[6] *Ibid.* p. 14.   [7] *Auban*, p. 5.
[8] Cf. Meyer, *Bozon*, p. lxv.   [9] Cf. Meyer, *Rom.* XXV, 255.

and the like. Again, when the *e* is not dropped we find *ensement* : *diseient*, 252, *forment* : *disoient*, 275; or the rhyming of preterite and imperfect; as, *crierent* : *disoient*, 289, *crierent* : *teneint*, etc. We have already noted a similar oxytone accentuation for the -*ent* of the present tense (cf. above, p. 122, 6).

65. IMPERFECT SUBJUNCTIVE.

Here, again, we have to call attention to the accent on the last syllable (*chantassént*). The phenomenon is by no means confined to Anglo-Norman, but is very frequent there [1] Under the influence of the accent the -*ent* may become -*ant* (*Soussant, Cumpoz* ; *veissant*, *Q. L R.*), and then -*ont* (*Dialogues Gregoire, rendissont, gardesont*, etc.[2]).

66. FUTURE.

This tense, in its various forms, illustrates several phenomena of Old French in general, as well as of Anglo-Norman. Some of these may be referred to, as follows: *tr, dr* > *rr, crerrat* (*Camb Psalt.*),[3] cf. above, p. 89; confusion of *rr* and *r, dirrai* (*Q. L R.*[4]), cf. above, p 89; fall of atonic *e* after a vowel, *envei-rai*, cf above, p. 63; fall of same after a consonant, *jurrez*,[5] cf. above, p. 64; insertion of *e* between consonant and *r, fauderai*, cf. above, p 90, 4, a; pretonic *i* > *e, vesterai, manterai*;[6] confusion of -*ai* and -*ei, servirei* (*Alexis*, L, str. 99), *Camb. Psalt. serei, chanterei*, XC, 15; CIII, 33; in this *Psalter* we notice a continuation of the -*ei* in the second person in *enseigneres*, CXVIII, 171.

67. PRETERITE.

Here we note a few isolated points, which we classify under the different types of the preterite.

1. -DEDI. The *Oxf. Psalt.* offers some of the rare examples which we have for the preservation of the old -*ie* :

---

[1] Cf. Meyer-Lubke, *Gram.* II, 388, § 307 ; Stimming, *Boeve*, p. lvi.

[2] Cloran, p. 60.   [3] Meyer-Lubke, *Gram* II, 396, § 314.

[4] Merwart, p. 9.   [5] Meyer-Lubke, *Gram.* II, 393, § 314.

[6] *Ibid* 395, § 314 ; Schlosser, *Q. L. R.* p. 57.

cunfundies espandies, espandierent.[1]   We note another case
in *Vie St. Edmond,* 2524, *espandie* : *lié.*

2. -s PRETERITE. Here are three noteworthy points.
First, the influence of the present on the preterite in forms
like *crienst, repunst, mainst* (in the *Psalters*).[2]   Second, the
confusion of *mest* (MANSIT) and *mist* (MISIT) which is peculiar to Norman and Anglo-Norman texts.[3]   Third, the extension of weak forms of this type (as *desis*) to regular weak
verbs; for example, *garesis* (for *garis*), *saisesis* (for *saisis*), etc.,
in the *Psalters* and *Q. L. R.*[4]   In the *Arundel Psalt.* we note
deguerpisis[5] (*fesis* occurs just before this), in *Vie St. Gilles,*
guaresis (3606), in *Sardenai* (L and O), *traisist* (98).   The
Anglo-Norman here furnishes examples of a phenomenon
not rare in general Old French.

3. -UI PRETERITE.   Here we call attention to the remark
of Paris[7] in comparing the forms *out* and *ot, plout* and *plot;*
out and *plout* represent the normal products, *ot* and *plot* the
abridged (cf. above, imperfect indicative, p. 123, 1).   These
perfects, *out, plout* are to be distinguished from those in -*ut*
(*aperceut, but,* etc.) which rhyme only with themselves.

4. -IERENT > -IRENT.   This change, in common with a
similar one of -*ie* to -*i* in infinitives and past participles, is
referred to in our next section (67).

5. -EUMES > -UMES.   On the fall of the atonic -*e* here (cf.
above, p. 60, § 17, 1, a).

6. -RÉNT.   For the oxytone here, cf. the remarks above on
the imperfect, p. 125, 3.

68. PAST PARTICIPLE.

We find quite a number of examples of the rhyming of
-*iée* (usually first reduced to -*ie*) and -*ie*; that is, to two

---

[1] Meyer-Lübke, *Gram.* II, 348, § 272.

[2] *Ibid.* 374, § 289.

[3] *Ibid.;* Schlösser, *Q. L. R.* p. 8.

[4] Meyer-Lübke, *Gram.* II, 375, § 289.   [5] *Zt.* XI, 521.

[6] *Ibid.* IV, 520.   [7] *Gme. de Berneville,* p. xxxiv.

rhyming in -*i* (*baissie* : *fie*). These are referred to by Stimming.[1]

69. MISCELLANEOUS, IRREGULAR OR PECULIAR FORMS.

We here append, in the alphabetical order of their infinitives, some striking forms of verbs which have been referred to in various places.

Avoir. *Avant* occurs for the present participle in the *Psalters*,[2] as *Camb. Psalt.* XXXVII, 14, *avanz.*

Connaitre. *Conissiez, coneissiez* occur in the *Camb. Psalt.* and *Q. L. R.*[3] I note a similar example of the pretonic *i* in *Vie St. Edmond*, of D. Pyramus, *alisum* (1660), *menisum* (1665). Forms with *que-* are seen in *Vie St. Gregoire*, as *quenoistras* (1723), *qenu* (1724).

Creire. We find *crei* as third singular preterite in *Vie St. Gilles*, 1. 3611.[4]

Dire. We find *disum* in *Cumpoz* and *Bestiaire.*[5] In *Vie St. Gregoire* we note *dierrei* (1867).

Ester. We have a present, *estait*, analogical to *vait* in *Cumpoz* and *Brandan*,[6] and a preterite *estout*, analogical to *out* in *Camb. Psalt.*, *Q. L. R.*, and *Brandan.*[7]

Être. We encounter several interesting forms here. For the infinitive we find in *Vie St. Gregoire istre* (1562). In the present tense, we note in *Alexis*, L (str. 44, e) *soi; su* for *sui* is of course common in Anglo-Norman, consequent upon the reduction of -*ui* to -*u* (cf. above, p. 80) For the first person plural we find *semes* in *Vie St. Gregoire* (2271). The rare *esmes* is said to be found only in Norman and Anglo-Norman texts.[8] Paris cites it for the *Vie St.*

---

[1] *Boeve*, p. 202.   [2] Meyer-Lubke, *Gram.* II, 247, § 183.

[3] Schlosser, *Q. L. R.* p. 52.

[4] This refrence is given (incorrectly) as line 3615 in *Rom.* XI, 59♦.

[5] Meyer-Lubke, *Gram.* II, 232, § 169.

[6] *Ibid.* II, 290, § 224.   [7] Schlosser, *Q. L. R.* p. 19.

[8] Meyer-Lubke, *Gram.* II, 281, § 211.

Gilles,[1] and says it is almost unknown after the twelfth century. He refers to Burguy,[2] who cites several examples of *esmes* (*eimes, ermes*). In *Vie St. Gilles*, line 504, we find the spelling *aimes*. I note also in the *Bible Fragment* (ll. 125 and 634) two cases of *eimes*.[3] For the present subjunctive I note *susums* in *Vie St. Edmond*, line 948. For the imperfect indicative we find an odd set of forms in the *Vie St. Gregoire*: *ereit, eroit, eroient;* they are numerous, found, however, by the side of the regular *ere, ert*. Meyer[4] says he has never seen these forms elsewhere. They are evident creations on -EBAM imperfects (one never finds *erot*). We note *esteum* in Chardri, *Jos.* 1712. For the future we see *ierc* in *Camb. Psalt.* CXLV, 1.

Faire. For *faimes* we refer to the note by Paris on *esmes*, just quoted. He refers to the examples previously given by himself,[5] and adds one from *Oxf. Psalt.* We note an example in the *Vie St. Gregoire*, 983, where the *faimes* has the sense of a subjunctive; a few lines above, 979, occurs *façons*. For *faisum*, cf. the note on *disum*, above. The forms of the future, *frai*, etc., are very frequent in Anglo-Norman cf. (above, p. 61, § 17, 1, b), but not confined to our dialect.[6]

Getter. For *gettre*, cf. above, p. 119, 3; for *jutta*, etc., cf. above, p. 62, 4, a.

Plaire. For the present subjunctive, *plaise* occurs already in the *Psalters*.

Pouvoir. In *Aspremont*, line 63, we find *poreir* for *poeir;*[8] this recalls the imperfect *poreint* of the *Pèlerinage*, line 511 (cf. above p. 91, 6). For the present participle we find *poant* in *Oxf. Psalt.*, but both *poant* and *puissant* in *Camb. Psalt.*[9]

---

[1] *Gme. de Berneville*, p. xviii.
[2] *Grammaire Langue d' Oïl*, I³, 269–270.
[3] *Rom.* XVI, 186 and 201.   [4] *Ibid.* XII, 201.
[5] *Accent Latin*, p. 71.   [6] Meyer-Lübke, *Gram.* II, 396, § 314.
[7] *Ibid.* 234, § 169.   [8] *Rom.* XII, 448.
[9] Meyer-Lübke, *Gram.* II, 248, § 183.

Prendre. Metathesis is here frequent. *pernons, pernez,* etc. (cf. above, p. 91, 5, a). These forms occur in Norman too.[1]

Savoir. I note *soi* for *sais* in *Mélanges*, V, 8.[2] Examples of *siez, siet* (SAPIS, SAPIT) are given by Sturzinger[3] I add three of *siet* from *Vie St. Thomas* (I, 94; II, 2, 16). No satisfactory explanation for these has been given.[4]

Trouver. I note *troffe* as present subjunctive in *Sardenai* (O).[5]

[1] Meyer-Lubke, *Gram.* II, 257, § 189 , *Litblt* V, 69.

[2] *Rom.* IV, 377   [3] *Orthographia Gallica*, p. 39.

[4] Meyer-Lubke, *Gram.* II, 306, § 243.   [5] *Rom.* XIV, 91.

K

TEXT SELECTIONS

IT is not my purpose to make text selections a feature of
my completed *Manual ;* but on account of the peculiar interest of the Anglo-Norman dialect, both for students of English and of French, it has seemed desirable to add some
representative readings; these will facilitate the use of this
portion of the *Manual* for practical purposes. In many cases
I have selected extracts from editions now difficult of access;
I have tried to choose extracts which illustrate phenomena
described on the pages preceding the present appendix. I
add, in the form of foot-notes, variant readings from the
manuscripts, suggestions of reviewers, and the like, so as to
furnish the student with somewhat of a critical apparatus
for his reading. In the case of poetry, I retain the original
numbering of the lines as found in the editions cited.

PHILIPPE DE THAÜN: CUMPOZ[1]

PROLOGUS

Philipes de Thaun
At fait une raisun
Pur pruveires guarnir
De la lei maintenir.
5   A sun uncle l'enveiet,
Que amender la deiet,
Se rien i at mesdit
En fait u en escrit,

1, Philippe *CLS*; taun *S.* — 5, le enveit *S.* — 6, le *LS*; deit *S.* —
7, Se il de rien ad m. *S.* — 8, v en f. v *S*; ne en fait ne *C.*

[1] Edition Mall, p. 1.

A Hunfrei de Thaun,
10 Le chapelain Yun
E seneschal le rei:
Iço vus di par mei.

Salutatio ad Patrem

Or oez sun sermun
Cum le met a raisun.
15 Icil Deus ki tut fist
E ki tuz jurz veir dist,
Il guart l'anme de tei,
Que il n'i ait desrei,
Qu'ele ne facet rien
20 U tuz juiz n'i ait bien,
Ne li seit purluignie
La joie apareilliee.
Maistre, un livre voil faire
E mult m'est a cuntraire
25 Que tant me sui targiet,
Que ne l'ai cumenciet,
Kar mult est necessaire
Cele ovre que voil faire;
E mult plusur clerc sunt
30 Ki grant busuin en unt,
Ki pur mei preierunt
E m'anme beneistrunt.
E sainz Augustins dit
La u fait sun escrit,

9, unfrei *C*, unfrai *L*, unfraid *V*; taun *S*. — 10, ydun *LV*, yhun *C*, yun *S*. — 11, Le chapelein *S*, lu *CL*. — 12, dit *LS*. — 14, Cumme *S*. — 15, E cil *C*, deu *S*. — 17, le alme *S*. — 18, ait ia d. *L*. — 19, face *LS*, fait *C* — 20, ni *S*, nen *L*, ne *C*. — 21, purluine *S*. — 22, apareille *S*. — 23, Mais un *L*. — 25, targe *L*, targiez *S* — 26, cummeciez *S*, acumencet *C*. — 27, ker *L*; necessaie *CS*. — 28, Cel *CL*, cel liure *S*. — 29, plusurs clers *CS*. — 30, Ke *S* — 31, prierunt *L*. — 33, saint *CS*; augustin *S*, austins *L*; le dit *LS*. — 34, u il f. *CL*.

35 U numet le librarie
  Ki mult est necessarie
  As pruveires guarnir
  De la lei maintenir:
  Iço fut li saltiers
40 E li antefiniers,
  Baptisteries, graels,
  Hymniers e li messels,
  Tropiers e leçunier
  E canes pur plaidier
45 A cels ki le mal funt,
  Envers Deu se forfunt,
  E cumpoz pur cunter
  E pur bien esguarder
  Les termes e les cles
50 E les festes anuels.
  Par ço devum guarder
  Nostre lei, celebrer
  Des Pasches, des Noels
  Les granz festes anuels.
55 U par cest les tendrunt,
  U viaz i faldrunt.
  D'iço me plaist guarnir
  Cels ki unt a tenir
  Nostre crestientet
60 Sulunc la Trinitet.
  Ço dit sainz Augustins,
  Ki fut mult bons divins,

35, libraire *S.* — 36, Ke *S.* — 38, A la *CL.* — 41, Baptisterie *CS*; grahels *C*, e graels *LS* — 42, Li hymners *C.* — 43, Tropeir *S*; lecuners *C*, leconiers, *L.* — 44, pur parlers *C*, porparliers *L.* — 46, Et vers deus *S.* — 47, cumpot *C*, compote *L*, compot *S.* — 49, clefs *L.* — 50, annuels *S.* — 51, Par cest *L*; deuuns *C.* — 52, e (et *S*) cel. *LS.* — 53, de noels *C.* — 54, Les] Des *CLS*; annuels *S.* — 55, le tendr. *L*; U par cez latendrunt *C*; par ceo les tendr. *S.* — 57, a guarn. *L.* — 58, Ces *C*, Ceals *L*, Icels *S*; lunt a t. *S.* — 59, cristientet (xpist. *L*) *CL.* — 61, dist *C*; saint *S*; austins *L.* — 62, bon *S*; devins *CLS.*

Avisunkes pot estre
Que il unkes seit prestre,
65 S'il ne set cest librarie
Dunt faz cest essemplarie.

REPREHENSIO ALLEGORICE PER PROVERBIA

Que ferat pasturel
Ki nen at nul drapel?
Cum guarderat berbiz
70 Ki nen at nul pastiz?
E Deus, cum cumbatrat
Ki ses armes nen at?
N'avum fei ne creance,
Ki doust estre lance
75 Cuntre cels enemis
Ki sur nus sunt espris.
Il pernent la citet,
Le mur unt enfundret,
Fait i unt grant baee,
80 Vunt i od grant huee.
Ço est pur le seignur
Ki se siet en la tur,
Ki ne se pot defendre
N'od els bataille prendre.
85 Cument pot hom loer
Que bien curget par mer
Nef, ki seit desquassee
E desuz enfundree?

64, il lacking *S* —65, siet *L*, libraire *S*. —66, dum faiz *C*, essamplaire *S*. —67, frat *S*. —69, cument *S*. —70, qui nen nad *C*, ki nad *S*. —74, Ke *S*; deust *L*, dust *S*. —75, c. noz *S* —77, prennent *C*; cite *CLS*. —78, effundre *C*, esfundre *L*, enfundre *S*. —79, Fait vnt *S*, Hardi unt *C*; baudee *S*. —80, Vunt lur huee *S*. —81, par *CL*; le lacking *S*. —82, Ki siet sus en *L*, qui set en *C*. —84, eals *L*; batailes *S*. —85, pot lom *L*. —86, Ki *L*, qui *C*; curt *C*, curge *L*. —87, Ke *S*; esquasse *S*. —88, desus *C*; enfundre *S*, esfundree *L*.

Dire ço pot li prestre :
90   Senz cumpot pot bien estre,
Bien set us de mustier
E ses festes nuncier.
E jo li respundrai
Par raisun e dirrai :
95   Hom set par us chanter
Cum esturnels parler.
Ne larrai nel vus die,
Nen est pas juglerie,
Ne n'est Grius ne Latins,
100   N'Hebreus ne Angevins,
Ainz est raisun mustree
De la nostre cuntree.
Bien poent retenir
Ço dunt jos voil guarnir,
105   Se il volent entendre
E bone guarde prendre.
Mais cuit qu'alquant dirrunt,
Ki puint de sens n'avrunt,
Qu'en vain me travaillai,
110   Quant cest livre ordenai ;
E jurrunt, pot cel estre,
Le vertuus celestre
Que unc ne soi rimer
Ne raisun ordener.

89, Dirre coe pot 1 p. *C* ; Dirra (Dirrat *S*) cupet li p. *LS*. —
90, pot lacking *S*. — 91, Bien ws set demustrer *S*. — 92, Ses festes
et denuncier *S*. — 93, lui *L*. — 94, et mustrai *S*. — 95, Hom *CL*,
Le *S*. — 96, Cum *S* ; e *C* ; et *L* ; asturnel *CS*, estornel *L*. — 97, lerrai
L ; nel *S*, ne *CL*. — 98, Ne est *C*, Nest *S*. — 99, griu *CLS*. —
100, Ne hebreu ne ang. *L*, Ne peitevins ne ang. *S*, ne nen est ang. *C*.
— 103, pot lem *S*. — 104, Co dunt vos v. *L*, Coe dum ges v. *C*,
Ceo dunt io v. *S*. — 105, atendre *S*. — 106, Et voilent g. p. *S*. —
107, M. quid qualquant *L*, Mais que que alq. *C*, Mais li quel ke d. *S*.
— 108, Ke *S*, ni *S*. — 111 E] lacking in all. — 112 Le *L*, Les *CS* ;
uertur *S*. — 113, rimeier *L*.

115   Mei ne chalt que fols die,
             Jo ne m'en repent mie;
             Asez sunt malparliers
             Pur mult petiz luiers
             E humes pur blasmer,
120   Neient pur amender.
             Unc pur fols nel truvai
             Ne ne m'i travaillai;
             N'unc ne fut asnes net
             Ki bien loast citet.

OXFORD PSALTER [1]

PSALMUS I

1. Beneurez li huem chi ne alat el conseil des feluns, & en la veie des peccheurs ne stóut, & en la chaére de pestilence ne sist

2. Mais en la lei de nostre Seignur lá voluntét de lui, & en la sue lei purpenserát par júrn é par núit.

3. Et íert ensement cume le fust quéd est plantét dejuste les decúrs des éwes, chi dunrát sun frut en sun tens

4. Et sá fúille ne decurrát, & tútes les coses que il unques ferát serúnt fait próspres.

5. Nient eissi li felun, nient eissi; mais ensement cume la puldre que li venz getet de la face de terre.

115, Mei ne chat *S*, Mais ne chalt *C*, Mais qui chalt *L*; fol *S*. — 116, Je *C*, men *S*, me *CL* — 117, Asunt *S*, mas parlers *C*. — 118, E pur *L*; mult lacking *C*; petit *S*; luers *CLS*. — 120, Naient *C*, Nient *S*, E nient *L*. — 121, Vnkes p. fol *S*. — 122, mi *CL*, men *S*. — 123, Ne ne fut *S*; asne *CLS*, ne *LS*. — 124, cite *LS*.

Variants (given by Michel)

Cod Cott 1 Beonure barun cunseil. et pecheurs et. 2. Seignor la volunted, e *Deest* de lui 3. E. ki. froit. son. 4 E e ferad

[1] Edition Michel, pp 1 and 212. The accent marks in the first psalm I take from the copy in Bartsch, *Chrestomathie*, 7th ed , col. 53

6. Empuríce ne resurdent li felun en juíse, ne li pecheur el conseil des dreituríers.

7. Kar nostre Sire cunúist la véie des jústes, é le eire des felúns perirát.

PSALMUS CXXXVI

1. Sur les flums de Babilone, iluec seimes e plorames, dementres que nus recordiums de Syon.

2. Es salz els milliu de li, suspendimes noz organes.

3. Kar iluec demanderent nus, chi chaitis menerent nus, paroles de canz;

4. E chi menerent nus : Loenge cantez à nus, des canz de Syon.

5. Cument canterum-nus le cant del Segnor en estrange terre ?

6. Si je oblierai tei, Jerusalem, à obliance seit dunée la meie destre.

7. Aerde la meie langue as meies jodes, si mei ne rememberra de tei;

8. Si je ne proposerai Jerusalem el cumencement de la meie ledece.

9. Remembrere seies, Sire, des filz Edom, el jur de Jerusalem;

10. Chi dient: Voidez, voidez, desque al fundament en li.

Variants

Cod. Cott. — 6. Empuriço ne surdent. pecheor. 7. l'eire.

Cod. Cott 1. Babylonie 3. caitis. chanz. 4. E chi ki. 7. remembera. 8. al. leece. 10. fundement.

Psalt. Corb. 1. Babylonie, iloec. recordiuns 2. de millui de lui. 3. ki caitifs m. voz p. 4. E ki en veie menerent nus : L. c. à n., de c. de S. 5 C. c.-n. del Seignur. *Desunt* le cant. 6. Se jo. e à o donée. 7. Aerdet. à mes joes, se m. ne rememberat. 8. So jo ne purposerai. comencement. leece. 10. Ki d. : Voidient, v., d. el.

11. Fille de Babilone caitive; beneurez chi redunrad à tei la tue gueredunance, laquele tu regueredunas à nus.

12. Beneurez chi tendra, e esgenera les tues[1] enfanz à la pierre.

CAMBRIDGE PSALTER[2]

PSALMUS I

1. Beoneuret li heom ki ne alat el cunseil de feluns, e en la veie des pecheurs ne stout, e en la chaere des escharniseurs ne sist.

2. Mais en la lei del Seignur la volentet de lui, e en la lei de lui penserat par jur e par nuit.

3. E iert ensement cume fust tresplantet dejuste les ruisals des ewes, lequel sun fruit durrat en sun tens.

4. E la foille de lui ne decurrat, e tuit ceo que il ferat serat feit prospre.

5. Nien issi felun, mais ensement cume puldre, lequel degetet li venz.

6. Pur ceo ne resurdrunt li felun el juise, ne li pecheur en la asemblée des justes.

7. Kar cuneut li Sires la veie des justes, e l'eire des feluns perirat.

Variants

Cod. Cott 11. Babylonie redunrat. reguerredunas. 12 esgerera. tuens

Psalt. Corb. 11. Babilonie ki reguerdonerat guerredonance. guerdunas. 12. ki tendrat, e esgenerat l. suens emfanz.

Variants (given by Michel)

1. conseil de 2. Meis Seinur la voluntet. 4. serrat fait. 5. Nient. meis. 6. assemblée.

[1] Meister collation : tuens
[2] Edition Michel, pp. 1 and 244

1. Sur les fluez de Babiloine, iluec sesimes e plourames, cum nus recordissums de Sion.

2. Sur les salz en miliu de li, suspendimes noz estrumenz.

3. Ker iluec nuns demandowent ki chaitifs nuns menerent, paroles de chançun; e cil ki nuns tormentowent: Lié, chantez a nuns des chanz de Sion.

4. Cumment chanterums la cantike Damne-Deu, en aliiene terre ?

5. Se jeo serai oubliez de tei, Jerussalem, en oubliance seit ma destre.

6. La meie langue aherged a mun guitrun, se jeo ne me recorderai de tei, se jeo devant ne metrai Jerussalem en l' comencement de ma leece.

7. Remembre te, Sire, des filz Edom el jurn de Jerussalem, des disanz: Esfowed, esfowed juske al fundement de li.

8. La fille Babiloine deguastée; boneûred ki guerdunerad a tei la twe feiede, ke tu guerdunas a nuns.

9. Bunewred ki tendrad, e ahurterad ses petiz enfanz a la pierre.

QUATRE LIVRES DES ROIS[1]

LI QUARZ LIVRES DES REIS

.XXV.

Al nuefme an lu rei Sédéchie, el disme meis, el disme jur del meis, vint Nabugodonosor li reis de Babilonie à tute se ost à Jérusalem, si l' aséjad e·ses engins i levad.

Mais cil dedenz tindrent la cited jesque al unzime an lu rei Sédéchie, le nofme jur del meis.

Lores i fud la famine tant grande que tenir ne porent la cited,[2]

---

[1] Edition Le Roux, p. 434.

[2] What Ollerich calls " Moderne Hand " here substitutes cit·ed.

Si s'enfuirent[1] nuitantre cez ki dedenz erent, e cil de Chaldée furent[2] à siége, e li reis Sédéchias s'enfuid[3] par la champaine del désert,

E li oz de Chaldée le sout, si l' pursewid, e prist e retint ès plaine[4] de Jéricho, e tuz ses hummes s'enfuirent,[5]

Si l' guerpirent en champ, e cil menèrent lu rei Sédéchie devant le rei de Babilonie à Antioche;[6] e li reis de Babilonie

Fist devant li[7] meime ses fiz ocire, e ses oilz crever, e de chaene[8] le fist lier e en Babilonie mener.

El quint meis e el setme jur del meis, ço fud li dise-nofme an[9] del règne lu rei de Babilonie que Nabuzardan li cunestable[10] de la chevalerie de Babilonie vint à Jérusalem;

E tuchad le fu e arst lu temple nostre Seignur, e le palais lu rei, e tute la cited;[11]

E fist les murs de tutes parz agraventer,

E les remasilles del pople ki furent là remès, e ki fuid s'en furent al rei de Babilonie, e les altres qu'il truvad tuz menad en chaitivier en Babilonie;

Mais del poverin de la terre i laissad partie que il s'entreméissent de la guaignerie.

Lores prist les riches columpnes de araim ki al temple furent od tutes les basses[12] e lu vaissele[13] ki fud el temple, de argent e de araim; e tant i out que l'um[14] ne sout lu peis.

E Nabuzardan prist les pruveires e les trésoriers del temple, e un des cunestables e des privez lu rei, e altres une masse, si's enveiad en Antioche al rei.

E là les fist ocire li reis, e jetad cez de Juda hors de lur pais.

---

[1] Ollerich's collation : s'en fuirent.   [2] Ollerich : i furent.
[3] Ollerich : s'en fuid.   [4] Ollerich plaines
[5] Ollerich s'en fuirent   [6] Modern hand : antiochie.
[7] Modern hand : lui.   [8] Ollerich . chaenes.
[9] Ollerich : ans   [10] Ollerich : cunestables.
[11] What Ollerich calls " Zweite Hand " here substitutes cit'ed.
[12] Zweite hand : ba'ses.   [13] Ollerich : vaissel.   [14] Ollerich : lŭ.

Si fist Godolie le fiz Aica le fiz Sapha maistre sur tant de frapin cume en la terre remest.

Cume li paisant surent que li reis Nabugodonosor out fait Godolie maistre de la terre, Ismael le fiz Natanie, e Johannan li fiz Carée, e Saraia li fiz Thenamech, e Jéchonias li fiz Machati, e lur cumpaignuns vindrent à lui en Masphath.

E Godolias lur fist serement que mal ne lur freit, si lur dist: Mar averez pour de servir à cez de Caldée; en ceste terre remanez, e le rei de Babilonie servez, e bien vus esterrad. . . .

BRANDAN[1]

> Donna aaliz la ʳeíne
> Par qⁱ ualdrát lei dívíné
> Par qⁱ creistrat lei de terré
> E remandrat tante guerré
> 5 Por les armes henri lurei
> E par le cunseil qⁱ ert entei
> Saluet tei mil emíl feixᶻ
> Li apostoiles danz benediz.
> Que comandas óó ad enpⁱs
> 10 Secund sun sens entre Mis
> En letᵉ Mis & en romanz
> Esi cū fud li teons cumanz
> De saínt Brendan le bon abeth
> Mais tul defent ne seit gabeth.
> 15 Qᵉnt dit qᵉ set e fait qᵉ peot
> Jtel seruant blasmer ne steot
> Mais si qⁱ peot ene uoile

Variants (from Oxford Ms. given by Suchier)

1, Donna aaliz] De ma halt. — 2, ualdra. — 4, remeíndra. — 5, Par. le. — 6, conseil. de tei. — 7, Salue. — 8, li apostolies donz beneiz. — 9, commandas. — 10, Si cum. en letre. — 11, romans. — 12, issi. fut (usually found). tuens. — 13, brandan. abet. — 14, tu le defende. gabet. — 15, poet. — 16, seriant. stuet. — 17, cil. puet. uoillet.

[1] Edition Suchier, *Romanische Studien*, I, 567.

Dreiz est q^e cil mult se doile
Jcist seínz deu fud ne$d$ de reis
20 De naisance fud des ireis
Pur ćó q^e fud de regal lín
Pur oc entent a noble fín
Ben sout q^e lesc^{l}pture dit
Ki de cest mund fuit de delit
25 Od deu de cel tant en aurat
Que pl^9 demander ne saurat
Puf oc guerpit cist reials eırs
Les fals honurs p^o iceals ueirs
Dras des Moíne pur estre vil.
30 En cest secle cū en eisil
Prist elordre eles habiz
Pu^{l}s fud abes par force eslız
Par art de liú mult iuíndrent
Qui ale ordre bein se tíndrent
35 Tres Mıl suz luí par díuers leus
Muníes aueit b^{a}ndan li pius.
De luí $p$nanz tuz ensample
Par sa vertud q^e ert ample
Li abes brendan p^{l}st enp^{s}pens
40 Cū home q^l ert de Mult g^{a}nt sens
De g^{a}nz cunseilz e de rustes
Cū cıl q^l ert for$\overline{m}$t iustes
De deu p^{l}er ne fereit fin
Pur sei ep^9 trestut sun lín.
45 E p^o les morz ep^o les uifs

Variants (from Oxford Ms given by Suchier)

18, mult se doile] puıs sen duıllet. — 19, fu neiz. — 20, naissance
fu de. — 21, ceo (usually so written). fu. reial. — 22, Pur oc] de
mıelz. — 23 [B]ıen. la scrıpture. — 24, fuıet le. — 25, ciel aura —
26, demander plus. saur$a$. — 27, cıst (lacking). — 28, le. onurs. ices.
29, m[u]ınie. — 30, icest siecle — 31, abiz. — 32, fu abez. — 34, ki
(usual) alordre bien. — 36, brandans. — 37, tous. — 38, anple. —
39, brandans. — 41, conseilz. — 43, feseıt. — 45, [mor]s.

Quer astrestuz ert amís
Mais de une en li p'st talent
Dunt deu p'er p'nt pl⁹ suuent
Que luí mustrat cel parais
50   V adam fud p'mes asis
Jcel q' est nost⁰ heritet
Dun nus fumes deseritet
Bien creit q' leoc ad g⁰nt glorie
Si cū nus dit ueire storie
55   Mais nep⁵tant uoldret uethe'r
V il deureit par dreit setheir
Mais par peccet adā for⁰st
P⁵ quei z sei nus fors míst
Deu en p'et tenablement
60   Cel luí mustret ueablement
Aínz q'l murget uoldreit uetheir
Quel sed li bon deurunt aueir
Quel lu le' mal aueir deurunt
Quel merite il receurunt
65   Enfern pried uetheir oueoc
E quels peín⁰s aurunt ileoc
Jcil felun q' par orguíl
Jci prennent par eols escuil.
De gurrer deu e la lei
70   Ne ent⁰ eols nen unt amur ne fai
Jéó dunt luí p's est desir
Voldrat Brandans par^{deu} sentir
Od sei p'mes cunseilz en p⁰nt
Qua un deu serf 9fesse rent
75   Barínz out nun cil ermíte
Murs aut bons esaínt uitté
Li fedeilz deu en bois estout
Tres cenz moínes od luí out

Variants (from Oxford Ms. given by Suchier)

56, [s]eier. — 60, [u]isablement. — 62, deuront. — 66, iluec. —
68, e[scu]el. — 70, fei. — 76, sainte uie. — 78, aueit.

De lei pᵉndrat conseil elos
80   De lui uoldrat aueir ados
Cil li mustrat par plusurs diz
Beals ensāples ebons espiz
Quil il uít en mer z enterre
Qᵃnt son filiol alat querre
85   Co fud m'noc q' fud frerre
Del luí v cist abes ere.

GAIMAR[1]

Quinte iui apres reis Harold vint;
Contre Norreis bataille tint
5225   Co fu Harald fiz Godewine,
Ki des Norheis fit discipline.
Co fut al Punt de la Bataille :
Norreis tiouat, pernant almaille.
Li reis Harold donc les sewi,
5230   Ireement se combati.
Laltre Harald el champ oscist,
E de Tosti ensement fist.
Sur les Daneis out la victorie,
La gent del Suth sembla grant glorie.
5235   Mais hom ne sout conter demis
Cels kel champ furent oscis.
Totes les nefs, e lur herneis,
Ad feit saisir Harald li reis.

Variants (from Oxford Ms. given by Suchier)
81, S[il]. —82, respiz.

Variants

5223, Quart *H*, Haralt *D*, Harald *HL* —5225, le fiz *DL.* —
5227, le (for al). — 5228, aumaille *H.* —5229, siwit *D*, siwi *L*, suit
H; donc omitted, *H.* — 5230, Irousement *H.* — 5233, uictoire *D*;
Norois *H.* — 5234, de Sud *L*; gloire *D.* — 5235, demi *H.* —5236, Ces
D, Qui *H*; pais *LH.* — 5237, lur (for les) *H.* — 5238, Ad omitted *H.*

[1] Edition Hardy and Martin, I, 221.

Le fiz cel rei i fust troue:
5240   Cil fust a Harald amene.
Merci cria, treu pramist;
Haralde homage de li prist.
E de trestuz les remananz,
Prist bons ostages, e vaillanz;
5245   Od vint nefs les lessat aler:
Donc airent tant ke sunt en mer.
   Cinc iors apres sunt ariuez
Franceis, od bien vnze mil nefs,
A Hastinges, desur la mer:
5250   Iloc firent chastel fermer.
Li reis Harald quant il oi,
Leuesque Aldret ad donc saisi
Del grant auer e del herneis
Kil out conquis sur les Norreis.
5255   Merleswain donc i lessat;
Pur ost mander en Suth alad.
Cinc iurs i mist al asembler,
Mais ne pout gueres avner,
Pur la grant gent ki ert oscise,
5260   Quant des Norreis fist Deus justise.
Tresken Suthsexe Harald alat,
Tel gent cum pout od li menat.
Ses dous freres gent asemblerent;
A la bataille od lui alerent,
5265   Li uns fust Gerd, laltre Leswine,

Variants

5239, celui *DH* (for cel rei). — 5239 and 5240 omitted *L*. — 5240, Cel *D*, Si, *H.* — 5241, triu *H.* — 5243, tuz *H.* — 5244, bons omitted *H.* — 5246, font *H* (for airent). — 5248, bien omitted *H*; IX *H* (for unze); miliers *L* (for mil nefs). — 5251, co oid *D*, co oi *L*, ceo oit *H* (for il oi). — 5252, Alred *DLH*; i *H* (for ad). — 5253, de *D.* — 5254, des *H* (for sur les). — 5255, idunc *DH.* — 5256, el *H.* — 5259, quot *D* (for ki ert). — 5261, Sudreie *L.* — 5262, Tant *D*, Tels *L*, Tieus *H* (for Tel gent); cum sei *D*; od sei *L.* — 5263, Les; genz *D.* — 5265, Gered *L*, Gerard *H*; Lefwine *D.* —

Contre la gent de vltre marine.

Quant les escheles sunt rengees,
E del ferir aparillees,
Mult ı out genz dambesdous parz;
5270 De hardement semblent leoparz.
Vn des Franceis donc se hasta,
Deuant les altres cheualcha.
Taillefer ert cil apelez,
Ioglere estait, hardi asez.
5275 Armes aueit e bon cheual:
Si ert hardiz e noble vassal.
Deuant les altres cil se mist;
Deuant Engleis merueilles fist.
Sa lance prıst par le tuet,
5280 Com si co fust vn bastunet:
Encontre mont halt le geta,
E par le fer receue la.
Traıs fez issı geta sa lance;
La quarte feiz, mult pres sauance,
5285 Entre les Engleis la lanca,
Par mi le cors vn en naffra.
Puis treist sespee, arere vint,
Geta sespee, kıl tint,
Encontre mont puis la receit.
5290 Lun dit al altre, kı co veit,
Ke co estait enchantement

Variants

5266, lost *H* (for la gent). — 5267, eschieles *D* , furent *LH*; rengies
D. — 5269, dambes *DH*, damp *L*. — 5270, leuparz *DL*. — 5273, Taill-
lifer *D*, Talıfer *H*. — 5274, Iuglere *DLH*; ert *DL*, omıtted *H*; ardız
D, hardiz *L* — 5276, bon *L* (for noble). — 5277, cıl omıtted *H*. —
5279, cuet *D*, cued *L*. — 5280, Sı cum *D*, Si come *H*, hastuned
L. — 5281, lengetta *H*. — 5282, sa (for la). — 5284, mult omıtted *H*;
par *L*, puis *H* (for pres) — 5285, la omitted *L*. — 5286, naurat *D*,
nauera *H*. — 5287, 5288, lespee *DH*. — 5288, Et geta *H*. — 5289, halt
DL, haut *H* (for puis); le (for la) *DH*.

L

Ke cil fesait, deuant la gent.
Quant treis faiz out gete lespee,
Le cheual, od gule baiee,
5295   Vers les Engleis vint a esleise,
Si i ad alquanz ki quident estre mange,
Pur le cheual ki issi baiout,
Le iugleor apris li out.
Del espee fiert vn Engleis;
5300   Le poing li fait voler maneis.
Altre en fiert tant cum il pout:
Mal guerdon le ior en out.
Car les Engleis, de totes parz,
Li lancent gauelocs e darz.
5305   Lui oscistrent, e son destrer:
Mar demanda le colp primer.
Apres i co Franceis requerent,
E les Engleis en contre fierent.
La out asez leue grant cri:
5310   Desci'kal vespre ne failli,
Ne le ferir, ne le lancer:
Mult i aut mort maint cheualer;
Nes sai nomer, nos mentir,
Lesquels alerent mielz ferir.

Variants

5292, Cil se fiert *H* (for Ke cil fesait).—5294, ad la *DLH* (for od).—5295, a omitted *DLH*; eslessie *D*, eslesse *H*.—5296, Alquant *D*, Alquanz *L*, Auquanz *H* (for Si . . . ki).—5297, si *DL.*—5298, enpres venout *H.*—5299, espie *D.*—5300, puin *D*, poin *L*, poign *H*; des mains *L* (for maneis), demanois *H.*—5301, Vn altre *H.*—5304, launcerent.—5305, Si l *H.*—5306, cop *DL*, coup *H.*—5307, requierent *DL*, les requierent *H.*—5309, Assez i out *H.*—5313, Ne *D*; ne ruis *DH*, rois *L* (for nos).—5314, Li Englois alerent bien ferir *H.*

ADGAR [1]

Vns moines ert Eueshamneis,
Ki mut ama Deu e ses leis.
La mere Deu reserui bien
E honura sur tute rien.

5 Ne laissa rien en nule guise,
Qu'apartenist a son seruise
Puis quant cil bers deueit murir,
A sei uit mut diables uenir.
Cuiluert erent e mult engres;

10 Deuant sei les uit ester pres.
Mais quant ewe beneite esteit
Getee, cum l'en faire deit,
S'en fuirent tuit li felun
De tutes parz de la meisun.

15 E puis tut dreit, cum dut murir,
La Dame uit a sei uenir;
La chere mere al Salueur
Dist li : "Ami, ne aies pour !
Ensemble od mei t'alme merrai;

20 En ioie, en repos la metrai !"
Cil la prist dunc a saluer
E icest respuns a chanter :
"Gaude, Maria; virgo chere !"
E rendi l'alme en ioie entiere.

25 Cum li respuns esteit pardit,
El ciel tramist son esperit.
Bien deiuent Crestien trestuit
Seruir la Dame e ior e nuit,
Asaier,[2] cumfaitement

30 Peussent faire sun duz talent;
Ne mie sulement li grant,

---

[1] Edition Neuhaus, p. 151.

[2] Foerster (corrections added to the edition, p. 251) suggests : *E asaier* as a probability.

　　　Mais fol e sage e nunsauant.
　　　A tuz rent bien sulunc merite;
　　　Plusurs defent de mort subite.
35　　E se il en muerent de tele mort,
　　　As almes rent ele grant cumfort,
　　　Cum ele fist a l'alme de un moine,
　　　Ki ert d'un mostier de Burgoine. —
　　　Deu nus duinst des pechez pardun
40　　Par fei e par comfessiun.

FANTOSME[1]

　　　Li sires d'Engleterre ad en sun cuer pesance
　　　Quant sun fiz le guerreie, qu'il nurri ad d'enfance,
80　　E veit que cil de Flandres l'unt mis en errance.
　　　Pramis li unt la terre des Engleis à fiance;
　　　Mielz volsist mort que vie qu'il eust la puissance,
　　　Tant cum il pout d'espée ferir u de lance.
　　　Establist sun barnage par fiere cuntenance,
85　　Vait encuntre Lowis, le riche rei de France,
　　　Cuntre le cunte Phelippun, dunt vus oiez parlance,
　　　E dan Maheu sun frere, chevalier de vaillance.
　　　Mult aida Deu le pere le jor, quant il l'avance,
　　　E mustra de sa guerre bele signifiance;
90　　Que le sucurs de sun fiz, ù plus fud s'esperance,
　　　Fud le jor agraventé senz nule demurance.
　　　Ço fud Maheu le puigneur, sur qui vint la lance;
　　　N'aurad mès li reis Henriz pur lui nule dutance.
　　　Li cuens de Buluine ad receu mortel plaie,
95　　De si qu'as espuruns à or li sanc vermeilz li raie.
　　　Ne purrad jamès guarir, asez ad qu'il asaie.
　　　Tant est sis freres plus dolent, e plus suvent s'esmaie,

Variants

78, quor pensance L. — 80, 81 omitted in L. — 83, peust, de sa lance L. — 87, En L. — 90, ot sa fiance L. — 92, Ceo fu L. — 96, ad assez L.

[1] Edition Howlett, p. 208.

E jure sun serrement, "La pretiuse plaie,"
Jamès vers le rei Henri n'aurad nule appaie.
100   Ore chevalche Lowis, si fait le jofne rei,
E Phelippe de Flandres est mis en grant desrei.
Li cuens Tiebaut de France demeine grant podnei.
Jà saverad li reis Henri asez ù mover sei.
Franceis li muevent guerre, Flameng et Cupei,
105   Li cuens de Leircestre, si i sunt ses fiz tut trei.
Icil de Tankarvile ne l'aime pas de fei;
Cent chevaliers à armes ameine en sun cunrei,
Ki tuit lui sul manacent de mettre en tel desrei
Ne li larrunt de teire le pris d'un palefrei.
110   Seignurs, en la meie fei, merveille est mult grant.
Pur quei li suen demeine le vunt si demenant,
Le plus honurable e le plus cunquerant
Que fust en nule terre puis le tens Moysant,
Fors sulement li reis Charle, ki poesté fud grant
115   Par les dudze cumpaignuns, Olivier, e Rodlant.
    Si ne fud mès oï en fable ne en geste
Un sul rei de sa valur ne de sa grant poeste.
Purquant lui vunt tuz maneçant, il en jure sa teste
Ne larrad pur riveier ne pur chacier sa beste.
120   Or chevalche li cuens Phelipe ovoc sa grant cumpaigne,
E guaste Normendie par bois e par champaigne.
N'en oissiez le rei Henri qu'il une feiz s'en plaigne,
Ne querre nul achaisun que la guerre remaigne.
Mult ad li juesne reis espleitié, qui si bien se baigne
125   Encore en ad les mandemenz des baruns de Bretaine.

99, n'avera nul apaie *L.* — 100, reis *L.* — 101, de Flandres *L*,
omitted *D.* — 102, Tebaud — pothnei *L.* — 105, Leecestre, si sunt *L.*
— 106, Tankervile. — 107, en meine a sun cunrei. — 110, mei, en est
L — 111, manaçant *L.* — 112, e plus cumquerant *L.* — 115, Oliver e
Rolant *L.* — 116, Ce ne fud (by erasure) *L.* — 118, li vunt manaçant
si en jure *L.* — 120, od sa grant cumpainie *L.* — 121, campaignie
L. — 122, que une feiz se plaine *L.* — 123, remaignie *L.* — 125,
Vncore *L.*

ANGIER (*Vie de Saint Grégoire*)[1]

Icist Eleuthere par nom
Un mort jadis resuscita,
324   E por itant lu amena
A cele houre, ovec sei, Gregoire
Privéement en l'oratoire;
Si l'en requist, por Dé amor,
328   Q'orast por lui Deu, q'icel jor
Veaus non trespasser lu donast
Q'od les enfanz lu jeunast;
Mais ne demoura fors brefment
332   Pues q'is orent ensemblement
Amdui, tant com lor plot, oré,
Quant Gregoires li ami Dé
Tant fort e legier sei sentit
336   Qe s'il vousist sanz nul respit
Jeuner jesq'a l'endemain,
Tant sei sentit vigrous e sein,
Bien lu pot faire sanz nul gref
340   Del mal del ventre ne del chief,
Si q'il soi merveilla de sei
Comment ço pot estre e par qei
Q'il ne mangot com il seut faire.
344   Ne voeil d'iço plus avant traire,
Car il meïsme asez reconte
A quei cele aventure amonte
Enz el tierz livre renomé
348   Del Dialoge translaté,
La ou par sa raison escleire
Les vertuz del dit Eleutheire.
Ço poet asez chasqun voier,
352   Por q'il voilge tant travaillier
Q'iloec en dreit lu deinge querre.

1 Edition P. Meyer, *Rom.* XII, 156.

Mais iceste avant dite guerre
La quele encontre sei enpiist,
356 Ja seit grant ennui lu feist,
Onc por ço ne fut plus oisdif,
Ainceis ert tant plus ententif
Nut e jor d'orer e de lire,
360 Ou d'estudier, ou d'escrire,
Si q'onqes ne cessa nule hore.
Qei feroie plus de demore
De reconter com pues vesqit,
364 Com nostre Sire lu rendit
Por son servise sa merite ? —
Gregoire en cele iglise ainz dite
Lonc tens tot aresié maneit
368 Ou de cru leum lu pesseit
La seinte Silvia sa mere,
Quant un jor en guise d'un frere
Lui trovot un angle escrivant
372 Qui bien resemblot par semblant
Uns oem qui fust de mer jeté,
De peril de mort eschapé,
La nef de qui fust perillée,
376 Par tempeste de mer brisée.
Cist itel lu appareisseit
La ou par costume escriveit.
Si lu requist por Dé amor
380 Q'eust merci de sa dolor,
Pitousement, od voiz plorable.
Gregoire qi fut merciable,
Douz, francs, pitous e deboneire
384 Tantost sanz demorer, en eire,
Sis deners trest de s'aumosnere,
Si lu donot od franche chiere;
E cil ilors graces rendant
388 Partit de lui liez e joant.
Mais ne demora fors briefment,

Quant eis le vos tot freschement
Un autre jor a lui venir.
392 Si se perneit a dementir
E se pleinst qe poi ot reçu
Encontre iço q'ot molt perdu;
E Gregoire erraument regiers
396 Lu donot sis de ses deniers
Doucement e de quer verai,
E li perillié sanz delai
Merciz rendant s'en vait joious.
400 Mais el tierz jor este le vous
Tot de novel par devant lui
Pleingnant e plorant a ennui,
Com s'il eust tot oblié
404 Quanq'il lu ot aincès doné,
E dist : "Por amor Dé, beau sire,
"Qui en son regne lu vos mire
"E por la salu de vostre emme
408 "Qe Deu la defende de blemme
"E de damage e de pecchié,
"Aiés merci del perillié,
"De ma mesaise, e de ma perte
412 "Qui tant par est dure e aperte
"Aiez, por siente charité,
"Compassion e pieté;
"Si me fai consolation
416 "De quei qe seit de vostre don,
"Dom mis doels seit asouagiez."
Gregoire atant s'est esbrusciez,
Com oem de charité espris,
420 Douz, merciable e francs e pis,
E dist a son chamberlenc lors:
"Va tost e sis deners onqors
"Lui aporte, si tu les as.
424 — Sire," fist s'il, "jo nes ai pas,
"Si Deu me saut, n'or ne argent

"Tant dom negun confortement
"Lu peusse a Oste hore faire."
428 Lors fut Gregoire en grant arvaire
Desquant soi vit en tel destreit,
Car d'une part pitous ereit
E d'autre triste e angoissous
432 Del povre qui vit soufreitous,
E de sa destresce demeine.
Neporquant a la fin aceine
Regiers son chamberlenc a soi,
436 Si lu dist: " Va tost, par ta foi,
" Si cerche par trestot laienz
" Huges, almaires, vestimenz,
" Si riens par aventure i truisses
440 " Dom lu reconforter peusses,
" Q'il ne s'en aut triste e plorant."
Atant respondit li servant:
" Sire, sachez qe dès piece a
444 " Enquis ai trestot quanq'i a,
" Mais veirement dener ne maille
" N'i troefs ne nule rien qui vaille
" N'en robe, n'en veisselement,
448 " Estre l'escuéle d'argent
" La quele a vostre maladie
" De legun sovent replenie
" Vos tramet vostre bone mere.
452 —Donc," dist Gregoire, od bele here,
" Va donqes tost, e si l'aporte
" Al povre qui se desconforte,
" Q'is eit, seveaus, de tant solaz."
456 Ço q'il ot dit fut fait viaz
Einsi com il l'ot commandé,
E cil qui ert povre quidé
La reçut, s'accuillit sa voie
460 Graces rendant od molt grant joie,
Mais jo quit quant repeirira

De chef, rens maes ne li querra,
Ainceis lu voudra, sanz mentir,
464   Quanq'ainz lu a donné merir.
A quei vos tendroie lonc tens ?
Mais tant par eroit en toz sens
Gregoire espirez de vertuz,
468   De miracles seinz reqenuz
Enprès la visitation
De l'angle dom faz mention,
Qe tut cil qui od lui vivoient
472   Tot autritant lu redoutoient
Com s'il fust per a seint André
Qui de s'iglise ert avoué.

CHARDRI[1]

La Vie des Set Dormans

La vertu deu ki tuz jurs dure
E tuz jurs est certeine e pure
Ne deit pas trop estre celee.
Car quant il fet chaut u gelee,
5   Nues voler, escleir u vent,
De ceo n'unt merveille la gent,
Ne de la terre ne de la mer,
Pur ceo k'il sunt acustumer
De veer cele variance,
10   Cum deu le fet par sa pussance;
E ne puroec mut esbaifs
I serrium, se ententifs
Pussum estre del penser,

Variants (given by Koch, p. 189)

1, *LO* ke ; *L* tutjurz, *O* tutjurs; ibid. 2. —5, *O* Nuwes. —6, *L* De
ceo num m'ille, etc., *O* De ceo um merveyle. —7, *O* tere. —8, *O*, keil.

[1] Edition Koch, pp. 76 and 164.

E deu nus vousist itant tenser.
15   Ne purrum pas a chef venir,
Se deu nel vousist meintenir,[1]
Ki purreit or sanz encumbrer
Les esteiles del cel numbrer,
Ne la hautesce del firmament
20   Ki tant est cler e tant resplent,
E la laur de tut le munde
E de la mer ki est parfunde:[2]
Mut purreit ben esmerviller
Ki weres en vousist parler.
25   Mes nus en pensum mut petit,
Car aillurs avum le nostre afit
Enracine par giant folie
En mauveste e en tricherie.
Car d'autre penser n'avum cure
30   Fors de cele malaventure
K'en cest secle veum user.
Trop i delitum, seinnurs, muser,
Si n'avrum fors hunte e dulur
Pur teu penser a chef de tur.
35   Cil ki de quoer vout deus amer
E retrere vout del amer
De cest munt ki tant travaille,
Mut se delitera sanz faille
Des uvrainnes Jhesu Crist
40   K'uncore fet e tuz jurs fist.
Leal serra ki par teu penser

14, *L* E ren (or veu?) n'uousist, etc — 17, *LO* ore. — 22, *LO* ke. —
23, *L* purreit len. — 26, *L* aflit — 28, *O* mauveiste. — 30, *LO* For. —
31, *LO* ke en — 33, *LO* for. — 34, *O* tel au chef — 35, *O* ke deu. —
37, *O* ke. — 39, *O* overaynes — 40, *O* ke; *LO* unkore; *L* tutiurz,
O tuzjurs — 41, *LO* lel.

[1] Mussafia (*Zt.* III, 604) suggests a period at end of this line.
[2] Mussafia suggests an interrogation point here.

Lerra sa grant folie ester.
Pur teus curages tenir
E le ben k'en poet avenir,
45 Une aventure vus cunterai,
Dunt ja ren ne mentirai,
D'un miracle ke fist Jhesu,
Ki pitus est e tuz jurs fu.
Ki deus eime de bon curage
50 Or i tende, si fra ke sage.
Ne voil pas en fables d'Ovide,
Seinnurs, mettre mun estuide,
Ne ja, sachez, ne parlerum
Ne de Tristram ne de Galerun;
55 Ne de Renart ne de Hersente
Ne voil pas mettre m'entente,
Mes voil de deu e sa vertu,
Ki est pussant e tuz jurs fu,
E de ses seinz, les set Dormanz,
60 Ki tant furent resplendisanz
Devant la face Jhesu Crist.
Car si cum il est escrit
Vus en dirrai la verite
De chef en chef cum ad este.

Petit Plet

Tuz ne sunt pas amis verais
1630 Ki vus losengent, de deus en treis.
Ki beit e mangue a ta table

Variants

44, *O* ke peot. — 46, *L* ni. — 47, *L* Dun. — 48, *LO* tutjurs. —
49, *LO* aime. — 50, *O* Ore i antende; *L* frad. — 51, *L* touid'; *O* de
Ovyde. — 52, *O* seynurs. — 53, *LO* Renard. — 56, *O* maentente. —
58, *L* tutiurz, *O* tuziurs. — 59, *O* des ses, etc., les VII, D. —
60, *LO* ke.

1629, *OV* verray(i)s. — 1630, *OV* ke; *LO* dous; *O* u treys. —
1631, *O* Ke; *O* maniuwe.

Ne serra ami cuvenable,
Se essae nel as avant—
Mar le crerras ne tant ne quant!
1635 Car ceus ki plus vus promcttereint
A chef de tur vus decevreint.
Teus juent e bel vus rient,
Au paraler de vus mesdient.
Cil vus eiment e pres e loin,
1640 Mes il vus faudrunt au graut busoin
Ceo est l'amiste de main en main :
Tant as — tant vaus, e tant vus eim.
De teus en avrez vus asez,
Deske les eez ben espruvez.

GUILLAUME DE BERNEVILLE

La Vie de Saint Gile[1]

Gires est en la veie mis,
Gerpist sa terre e ses amis ;
Il nen ad n'or n'argent od sai,
Cheval ne mul ne palefrei ;
645 Il n'en porte ne veir ne gris,
Meis povres dras de petit pris ;
Meis Deus ki est riches d'aveir
Lui truverat sun estuveir.
Il ad tute la nuit erré ;
650 N'est merveille s'il est lassé:
N'ert pas a us d'aler a pé ;

1633, *LOV* Si assae ; *OV* avaunt — 1635, *O* ki plus promettrey-
ent, *V* ke uns pmett'unt. — 1636, *V* chif ; *L* deccuerint, *O* -eyent,
V deceverunt. — 1637, *O* Teus iuwent, *V* Teus venint. — 1638, *L* Al,
V A paraler. — 1639, *L* aiment. — 1640, *V* bosoign, *LOV* al. —
1641, C'est for Ms ceo est , *L* le , *LV* mein en mein. — 1624, *LO*
ai(y)m — 1644, *O* Deske vus eez, *V* Deskes.

Manuscript Readings
641, mise. — 649, tut. — 650, si est.

[1] Edition, Paris et Bos, pp. 20, 38, and 46.

Ne pur kant mult s'est efforcé,
Kar la gent dute de sa terre
Ke nel sivent e facent guerre.
655 E il si funt, plusurs parties
Vunt lur curlius e lur espies,
Quérent a munt, quérent a val,
Ambure a pé e a cheval;
Mei est avis k'en vein le funt:
660 Ja de lur olz meis nel verrunt.

Entre le Rodne e Munpellers
1230 Ert le pais large e pleners
De granz deserz e de boscages;
Assez i out bestes sauvages,
Urs e liuns e cers e deims,
Senglers, lehes e forz farrins,
1235 Olifans e bestes cornues,
Vivres e tygres e tortues,
Sagittaires e locervéres
E serpenz de mutes manéres.
Gires n'en prent nule pour,
1240 Einz se fie en sun bon seignur.
El bois entre ki mut fud grant
E veit le Rodne costeant:
Or en penst Deus par sa merci,
Car pur s'amur ad tut guerpi;
1245 Se il n'en prent de lui conrei,
Ne mangera, car il n'at quei:
Ne porte od sei ne pain ne vin
Dunt il se digne a cel matin,
Ne tant que vaille un hanetun
1250 Entre vitaille e guarisun.

Manuscript Readings
654, Ki. — 656, Unt. — 1230, &. — 1231, grant. — 1236, Urs e t. —
1243, peust. — 1247, uine. —

Seigneur, oez un bel miracle:
Iloc u ert en s'abitacle
1505 E en sa loge u il urout
E nostre seignur depreiout,
Si vit une bisse sauvage
Tut dreit errante a l'hermitage.
La bisse fud durement bele
1510 E vint tut dreit a la venele
Par la sente k'ele trovad:
Entre les branches se musçat,
Ne dutet pas, meis dreit enz veit.
Gros out le piz e plein de leit:
1515 As pez Gire se veit gesir,
Presente sei de lui servir.
Gires ad la bisse veue
Ki a ses pez est estendue:
Mult se feit lez, kar ben suschad
1520 Ke Dampne deus lui enveiad.
Tant cum iloc el desert fud,
Del leit de la bisse ad vescud.
Or escutez cum el le sert:
Le jor veit peistre enz el desert;
1525 Quant vent a l'ure de disgner,
Ne l'estot pas pur lui aler:
Ele set ben le terme e l'ure,
Si sachez bien plus ne demure
K'el n'en venge dreit a la fosse;
1530 Ele fud bele e grasse e grosse:
N'i out si bele en la contrée,
Ne ne serad ja meis trovée.
Gires li feit a une part

Manuscript Readings

1505, E wanting. — 1507, E si — 1509, f. mut d. — 1518, estendu.
— 1519, lez wanting. — 1521, iloc wanting. — 1523, ele. — 1529, Kele.
— 1530, gras. — 1531, Nout, contre. — 1533, le f.

Une logette en sun essart
1535   U gist la nuit pur la fraidure ;
L'endemain veit a sa pasture.
De tel conrei cum jo vus di
S'est li sers Deu vescu meint di :
Quant il ad pris tant cum li haite,
1540   Nen ad messaise ne suffreite.

VIE DE SAINT THOMAS[1]

FEUILLET II

Li apostoilles ad grant angoisse,
Suz ciel ne siet ke faire puisse.
E li messager [au] cuntraire,
4   Ore funt un, ore funt el traire.[2]
Mut avroit en quor pesance[3]
S'il curuçast le roi de France
E des Franceis la commune.
8   Ceste est de dous parties la une,
Mès ceste requiert dreiture,
Lei e leauté e mesure.
D'autre part li rois Henris,
12   De terre, de aveir poestifs,
Ove ses evesques e ses clers
Est tut encuntre e en travers.
Si li rois ne se entremette
16   Lowis, ne siet quant pès i mette,
Kar mult est de descreciun,
De mesure e de grant resun.

Manuscript Readings
1538, uesqui.

[1] Edition P. Meyer, p. 11.
[2] " Corr. *or* dans l'un des deux cas."
[3] " *en* ou *eu* ? "

BOEVE DE HAUMTONE[1]

XLVI

Li emfes vint devaunt le emperur a vis fer,
290   hardiement commença a parler:
"Entendez vers moi, beau duz sire cher,
ky *vus* dona congé cele dame acoler?
Ele est ma mere, ne *vus* enquer celer,
e kaunt a moi ne volez congé demaunder,
295   jeo *vus* frai sa amur mou cher achater;
rendez moi ma tere, jeo *vus* voil loer.

XLVII

Beau sire emperur," dist Boefs li sené,
"vus acolez ma mere estre mon congé;
mun pere, ke taunt amai, *vus* avez tué.
300   Pur ceo, sire, *vus* pri ke moi ma tere rendez,
que *vus* fausement tenez tut saunz ma voluntez."
Lui emperur respondi: "Fol, kar *vus* teisez!"

XLVIII

Boefs tost oist ceo ke l'emperur ad dist,
taunt avoit grant ire que tut le sanc li fremist;
305   hauce la massue, en le chef le ferist,
treis cops li dona e *treis* plaies li fist
e jure par dampnedeu e le seint espirist,
si il ne li rent sa tere, a mal hure le vit.

IL

Ly emperur chai sur la table paumé.
310   La dame se escrie: "Ceo tretur me pernez!"
Les uns de chevalers urent grant pitez
de Boefs, le enfaunt, si sont il levez,
ausi com pur li prendre s'i sunt pressez,
e li emfes est enter eus queintement eschapez.

[1] Edition Stimming, pp. 13 and 72.

M

L

315 A l'hostel son mestre s'en vint il coraunt.
Sabot li vist si le va demaundaunt:
"Dount venez vus, beau fiz, si fortement hastaunt?"
"De tuer mun parastre," ceo dist li enfaunt;
"treis plaies li donai, kar il me apella truaunt,
320 jammés ne garira par le men ascient."

A le paleis l'eveske sunt il pus alez.
L'eveske a dunc fu mult lez,
a muster sunt alé de Sent Trinitez.
1955 Josian la bele est pus baptisez.
A dunc fu l'Escopart si longe e si lee,

CXLI

Ke dedens le fons ne put entrer.
Un grant couve funt aparailer
tut plein de ewe pur li baptiser;
1960 vint homes i furent pur li sus lever,
mes entre els ne li point remuer.

CXLII

"Seynurs," dist l'Escopart, "pur nent traveilez.
Lessez moi entrer; vus me en sakerez."
Diunt les altres: "vus dite veritez."
1965 L'Escopart salt dedens joyns pez,
si ke a le funde est avalez,
si fu en la funte Guy nomez;
e l'ewe fu freyde si li ad refreydez.

CXLIII

L'Escopart comence a crier
1970 e l'eveske forement a ledenger:
"Ke est ceo?" fet il, "malveis velen berger,
mey volez vus en cest ewe neyer?

Trop su jeo crestien, lessez moi aler."
Saili est ha present hors, ne voit demorer.
1975   Ke dunc le veit nu les granz sauz aler,
il li sereyt a vis, ne vus quer celer,
ke il fust un deble ke vousist manger.

LE CHEVALIER, LA DAME ET LE CLERC[1]

      Ore est li seignur mal arivé
548   Kar batuz est de sa maisnée,
Li un fiert al chef li autre al cool;
Ore se tint il bien pui fol.
Blescié se sent, en haut escrie:
552   "Merci par Deu, ma duce amie,
"Si me ociez vus freiet mal.[2]
"Jeo sui vostre sengnur leal;
"Par mal conseil ai meserret."
556   La dame se feint mult coiucée,
Respondi com par (mult) grant irrur,
Ke ceo ne fud pas sun seignur,
Mès fud le clerjastre de la vile
560   Ke deceivre la quidout par gile:
"Mei quidout honir e mon baron."
Il osta dunc sun chaperun
E la dame le reconuht.
564   Tantost a ses pez coruht:
"Sire," dist ele, "pur Deu, merci!
"Ki vus quidout oie aver ici?
"Forfete me sui durement.
568   — Par foi," dist il, "nun estes nient,
"Mais durement grant gré vus sai;
"A tuz jors (le) meuz vus amerai,
"Vous avez feit com bone dame;
572   "E cele ke vus miht en blame
"De moi ne ert james amie."

---

[1] Edition P. Meyer, *Rom.* I, 86.   [2] "Corr. *ferez.*"

Sa soer tantost ad enchacie,
Ama sa femme, la tint plus chere
576 Kant servi li avoit en teu manere;
E sa femme après cel jor
Ama e cheri son seignur
Azzez plus [k'] unke mès ne fiht.
580 De sun peché penaunce prist,
Ama Deu sor t te rien,
Unc puis ne mespriht de rien.[1]
Lung tens vesqui en vie bone
584 Del païs dame e matrone,
E kant moruth la bone dame
A Deu rendi sus sa alme.[2]

PÈLERINAGE DE CHARLEMAGNE[3]

Sire dist carleɱ uolez en mes des gas
Ki en auez coisit cil recumēcerat
E dist hug' li forz ueez ci b'nard
765 Filz le 9te aimer ki de co se uātat
Q; ile gᵃnt ewe q̄ brut a cel ual
Q; il la freit eisir tute de sun canal
Entrer ē la citet cᵘre de tutes parz
Mai mames mūter ē mū pl⁹ halt palais
770 Q; nen pᵘrai decendre tresq; il cumādereit
Ore set li qn̄s bernard lui estut cuɱcer
E dist a carleɱ damne deu en p'ez
Il uent curāt al ewe si ad les quez seignez
Deus i fist miracles li glorius del cel
775 Q; tute la gᵃnt ewe fait isir de sun bied
Aspandere les cāps q̄ tuz le uirēt ben
Entrer ē la citez 7 emplir les celers
La gēt lui rei hug' 7 moiller 7 guaer
En la plus halte tᵘ li reis sen fuid a ped

---

[1] "Corr. *Unkes.*" [2] "Corr. *la sue a.*"
[3] Edition (3) Koschwitz, p. 44.

780 Desur un pin antif ∞ carl' al uıs fer
Il 7 li duze pers li barun cheualer
Prient dāpne Deu q¹ d' eauls ait pited
Desur un pin antif est carlemaines
Il 7 li duze per le gētes cūpaınes
785 Oit lu rei hug' sus ē la tᵘ deplaindre
Sun tresor li durat sil cūdurat ē f*nce
E deuēdrat ses homes de lui tēdrat sū regne
Q*nt lentend le*pere* pıtet ē a ml't g*nde
Enuers humilitet se deit eom bē ēfraindre
790 E p¹et a ihū q̄ cele ewe remaıgnet
Deus i fist g*nt u'tut pᵘ aınᵘ Carlemaıgne
Leue ist de la citet si sen vaıt *p* les plaines
Reētret ē sun canal les riues en sūt pleınes
Des put ben li reis ı⁹ de la tur decēdre
795 E uent a Carlem̄ desuz lūbre de une ente
A feiz dreız em*pere* io saı ke d's u' aıme
Tis hō uoil deuenir d' teı tēdraı mū regne
Mun tresor te durraı si fraı amener ē f*nce
Volez en mes des gas sıre dıst carlemaıne
800 E dist hug' li forz ne de ceste semaıne
Si tuz st' aāplı ıa ne ert ıur k; ne me plaigne.

BOZON [1]

Le corf porta un furmage en sa bouche, a ky le gopyl en-
countra; ci dit: "Dieux! Com vous estez beal oysel, e ben
seriez [2] a preiser, si vous chauntassez [3] auxi cler cum fist
jadys vostre pıere!" Le corf fust joyous del loenge, si overı
sa bouche pour chaunter, e pƈrdy soñ furmage. "Va tu,"
dit le gopil, "asez en ai de toñ chañt."

———

Un veox homme jadis out une joene femme. E pur
graund affiaunce qe out en lui, touz ces bienz a lui doɪa en

[1] Edıtion Smith et Meyer, pp 15, 44, 98, and 113.
[2] *A* serrettez.   [3] *B* chauntıssiez.

morrañt. Si la pria pur Dieu qe ele pensast de lui eyder après sa mort. "Volunters," fet [ele], "si voille Dieux!" Morust le sire e la femme prent un garceoñ qoynt vielours et assemee, taunt que un jour la femme envoya un presañt de payn e de cerveyse al chapelyn pur chañter pur la alme sa primer baroñ. L'autre vynt; si lui encontra e fist le present retorner. "Jeo say," dit il a sa femme, "meux chañter qe le chapeleyn. Emples deus hanapez, si irroms caroler. Le vaillard fui plus gelous de autres qe de sey, et jeo, qe sui estrange, quai frai jeo pur lui?"[1] Fols est qe se affie en autres après sa vie e lest sa alme nuwe pur mettre en estrange muwe. Ceo est a dire en engleys:

> He yat hadd inou to[2] help him self wital,
> Sithen he ne wold,[3] I ne wile ne I ne schal.

Un seint home qe fust appellé Carpe out tournee un mescreañt a la fei de seint Esglise. Et tant com fust hors du pays, celui returne a mescreaunce par coñseil de un mauveys home. Doñt seint Carp fust tant grevee de ceo e[4] a mal eese q'il pria a Dieux qe il preïst de eux vengeañce. E en poy de houre[5] lui fust a vys [en avision[6]] y'il vy enfern overir e ceo deuz prestez pur entrer. Et tant fust corucee vers lur peché qu il desira[7] qe eux fussent entrez. Lors appareust Jesu Crist od ses[8] playes totes sanglañtz, e dit a Carp: "Vers moy regardez e ma peyne avisez e de qeor[9] entendez ma[10] dolour qe jeo endurai[11] pur sauver pechour. Vous pernez a trop legier ceo qe me costa mout cher. Si autre foiz morir puse, com fere nel puis a nul feor, ma volenté serreit pur home morir, tant ay a[12] lui grand amur." Le seint home, après la vewe, se repenty, e pria Dieux pur les autres merci.

[1] _A_ qe fra pur lui qe fray. [2] _B_ til.
[3] _B_ adds for sothe. [4] _B_ omits grevee de ceo e.
[5] _B_ adds après. [6] _B._ [7] _A_ desirra.
[8] _B_ le. [9] _B_ omits de qeor. [10] _B_ la.
[11] _A_ endurrai. [12] _B_ vers.

Qui ad trop de chevux e veot estre allegee prenge le jus
de cardoñ e moille sa test, e il trovera allegeaunce a sa
volentee. Auxint vous di: qi est trop chargé de chateux
au des biens temporaux ou de deners, quierge l'amur de
felun seignur a sa ayuoy[n]tañce, e il serra deschargee.
Pur ceo dit le sage homme: "Ne vous aquoyntez pas al
riche," qar com plus lui donez plus te grevera.

FRÉDÉRIC MISTRAL, Poet and Leader in Provence

By CHARLES ALFRED DOWNER

*Assistant Professor in the French Language and Literature in the
College of the City of New York*

Cloth   12mo $1.50 *net*

" Professor Downer's book is the most important treatise on the subject that has yet appeared in English, and deserves commendation, not only for the story of the life of Mistral and its detailed examination of the merits and defects of his various compositions, but also for its statements of the chief phonetical, grammatical, and prosodical peculiarities of the Provençal language." — *The Independent.*

CORNEILLE AND THE SPANISH DRAMA

By J. B. SEGALL, Ph.D. (Columbia)

*Instructor in French in the College of the City of New York
Sometime Fellow in Romance Languages in Columbia University*

Cloth   12mo $1.50 *net*

" This is a brief but excellent work in which the author, after showing how greatly the literature of France of the sixteenth and seventeenth centuries was indebted to Spain, dwells especially on the overweening power of the Spanish stage over the French drama during the age of Corneille, and how the great French master borrowed plot and often thoughts and expressions from Spanish playwrights." — *The Arena.*

THE INDEBTEDNESS OF CHAUCER'S "TROILUS AND CRISEYDE" TO GUIDO DELLE COLONNE'S "HISTORIA TROJANA"

By GEORGE L. HAMILTON, A.M.

*Sometime Fellow in Columbia University
Professor of Romance Languages in Trinity College, North Carolina*

Cloth   12mo $1.25 *net*

One of the most interesting and disputed questions connected with the literary development of the Troy Legend is that of the sources of Chaucer's *Troilus and Criseyde.* Chaucer's general indebtedness, in this work, to Boccaccio's *Filostrato* is well known and has been sufficiently set forth. The present author, on the other hand, following out a new line of discovery, makes a careful and penetrating examination of the relations of the *Troilus and Criseyde* to Guido delle Colonne's translation, under the title of *Historia Trojana*, of Benoit de Sante-More's *Roman de Troie.* The method and results of Mr. Hamilton's study, as here presented, will be of interest alike to students of English and of Romance literature.

THE MACMILLAN COMPANY
66 FIFTH AVENUE, NEW YORK